EDITORIAL

I want to open this editorial with thanks to all readers and members for their patience as we bed down further systems and processes for publishing this and future issues of *Archives and Manuscripts* both online and in print.

In this issue, we see conversations about pushing boundaries in practice emerge, along with setting the scene for emerging scholarly and professional practices. In particular, I note that we are publishing the first scholarly article to use a Traditional Knowledge (TK) notice (Wilson & Barrowcliffe), something that is long awaited and that we will continue to refine and apply as the journal and TK systems grows. This issue also confirms what I hope to be an ongoing practice of practitioners sharing the experiences and reflections on their everyday work in what is a core profession for our society.

As Wilson and Barrowcliffe[1] outline, the challenges of sharing TK through publication in scholarly sites such as *Archives and Manuscripts* also creates opportunities to push boundaries. Their article includes a TK notice and I encourage you to read and reflect on the meaning this labeling gives to what you are reading. As an Editor I have worked closely with the authors and the Local Contexts team at New York University to apply these emerging labels, and it has been a productive and educational process. Of note for me is the way the labels worked to unsettle and challenge assumptions through most parts of the scholarly publishing process, from review through to copyediting and typesetting, and how this becomes productive to the whole process.

Also in this issue, Shani Crumpen[2] explores the role of Indigenous Data Governance in a community archives setting. Through the case study Crumpen traces the multiple sites and stakeholders in the community setting, and draws on her own experience and reflections to evaluate the role of Indigenous Data Governance and Sovereignty in this community setting. Crumpen finds that through realising Indigenous Data Governance there are opportunities to challenge institutional and other rigid frameworks, again encouraging boundaries to be shifted and renegotiated through archival practice.

Jennifer Douglas[3] then takes on a little studied and discussed area of archival practice – that of donor relations, extending her work from the previous issue of *Archives and Manuscripts* to acknowledge and symbolise the importance relationships archivists develop with donors, often over extended periods of time, and the manifest role of grief in these relationships. Similarly, Sarah Welland[4] takes us to an area that is under-discussed in practice – that of the role of the expert user in the archive, and the perception of purpose in light of these users. For both Douglas and Welland, these stakeholders play active and engaged roles in archival practices, and their research brings these roles to the fore.

This issue includes three reflections from practitioners that are themed around the audiovisual archive – Ben Pask's[5] reflection on working at the ABC News Libraries, Eva Samaras's[6] work on visual effects archiving, and Theresa Cronk's[7] report on the 'Music and the First World War' project at the Australian War Memorial. These three articles give an insight into the variety of work being done at national and international institutions that intersect with audiovisual records, and the importance of an experienced and committed workforce to support these unique and emerging records.

As we move slowly into a post-pandemic world and one where scholars and practitioners are more likely to be sharing spaces and networks again, I look forward to future special issues that bring these sometimes disparate groups together. Keep an eye out for an upcoming call for a special issue, and please continue to send through your thoughts and feedback on the journal.

Dr Jessie Lymn, Canberra, Australia
General Editor, *Archives and Manuscripts*

Notes

1. Leann Wilson and Rose Barrowcliffe, 'Green Ribbon and Blue Ribbon Stories: Applying a Bidjara Way of Knowing to Understanding Records', Archives & Manuscripts, vol. 50, no. 2, 2022, pp. 43–59. doi: 10.37683/asa.v50.10921.
2. Shani Crumpen, 'Realising Indigenous Data Governance: A Case Study of the Koori Resource and Information Centre Archives', Archives & Manuscripts, vol. 50, no. 2, 2022, pp. 3–21. doi: 10.37683/asa.v50.10213.
3. Jennifer Douglas, 'On 'Holding the Process': Paying Attention to the Relations Side of Donor Relations', Archives & Manuscripts, vol. 50, no. 2, 2022, pp. 23–42. doi: 10.37683/asa.v50.10925.
4. Sarah Welland, 'Created, Intended, Articulated and Projected: FourPerceptions of Purpose Around the Archival Document for Expert Users', Archives & Manuscripts, vol. 50, no. 2, 2022, pp. 61–75. doi: 10.37683/asa.v50.10919.
5. Benjamin Pask, 'Hunters and Collectors: The Work of ABC's News Libraries across Archives and TV News Production', Archives & Manuscripts, vol. 50, no. 2022, pp. 77–80. doi: 10.37683/asa.v50.10917.
6. Evanthia Samaras, 'Archiving Visual Effects: Filling a Digital Void in the Documented Memory of Film and Television', Archives & Manuscripts, vol. 50, no. 2, 2022, pp. 81–88. doi: 10.37683/asa.v50.10417.
7. Theresa Cronk, 'The Music and the First World War Project at the Australian War Memorial', Archives & Manuscripts, vol. 50, no. 2, 2022, pp. 89–101. doi: 10.37683/asa.v50.10913.

ARTICLE

Realising Indigenous Data Governance: A Case Study of the Koori Resource and Information Centre Archives

Shani Crumpen*

Department of Social Enquiry, La Trobe University, Melbourne, Australia

Abstract

This paper presents research findings from a study exploring how Indigenous community archives realise Indigenous Data Governance (ID-GOV). It considers the development of the Koori Resource and Information Centre (KRIC) Archives in Shepparton, Victoria, as a case study. This study aimed to determine whether the KRIC Archiving Project realised a form of ID-GOV. It adopted an Indigenous methodological framework using a combination of data collection methods to generate a range of research data. This study found that the KRIC Archiving Project adapted Western archival frameworks and practices to create an archive of local Indigenous significance and history that was accessed, operated and managed under Indigenous direction. In this way, the Project advanced Aboriginal and Torres Strait Islander self-determination and achieved a momentary emergence of ID-GOV.

Keywords: *Indigenous community archives; Indigenous Data Governance; Aboriginal and Torres Strait Islander; Self-determination.*

The movement for Indigenous Data Sovereignty (ID-SOV) and Indigenous Data Governance (ID-GOV) has emerged in response to poor data practices. Since colonisation, Indigenous lives have been heavily surveyed and documented in archival collections across Australia. Missing from these archives has been the inherent and undeniable voices of First Nations Australians regarding the collection, ownership, possession and management of data pertaining to their people, knowledge systems, way of life, lands and waters. An integral part of transforming the dominant discourse about current data development and management practices and archiving protocols is the privileging of Indigenous knowledge and culture. Although the histories and experiences of Indigenous lives vary at regional and national levels, they share common narratives of resilience and resistance to colonialism and frameworks of white hegemony.[1] This has seen the emergence of Indigenous community archives (ICAs), which adapt and transform rigid hegemonic structures to meet the specific needs of the community.

This paper is based on my study about the development of an ICA in an Australian context, focusing on the Koori Resource and Information Centre (KRIC) Archives in Shepparton,

*Correspondence: Shani Crumpen, Email: shani.crumpen@unimelb.edu.au

Victoria, as a case study.[2] The research sought to determine whether this particular ICA achieved ID-GOV. Its methodological approach was shaped by an Indigenous research paradigm to ensure that Indigenous perspectives and knowledge were foregrounded. A combination of data collection methods was used to produce a range of research data.

The term KRIC is applied in various ways throughout this article. Variants of the term include 'KRIC' or the 'KRIC office', which refers to the community organisation; the 'KRIC Archives', which refers to the community archive itself; and the 'KRIC Archiving Project', which refers to the management, sorting, cataloguing and preservation of the archival material.

Indigenous community archives

ICAs are not a recent phenomenon. As Baker & Cantillon argue, works undertaken by Indigenous communities to reclaim, repatriate, create and govern their 'memory, identity, knowledge, and culture pre-date … the community archive movement'.[3] The community archive movement evolved around the mid-1970s and early 1980s in response to protests of antiwar, civil rights, and gay and feminist activists.[4] The materials housed in ICAs comprise various types and forms of records that relate broadly to their respective communities, people, land and waters, histories, knowledge, language, and community organisations and initiatives.[5] Moreover, ICAs provide a space that gives voice to marginalised communities who are often excluded, silenced, othered and subjugated in colonial accounts.[6] In this regard, ICAs contest assumptions deemed as truths; challenge the 'hegemony of the nation-state's imagined past and futures; and invoke a multiethnic cacophony of voices that requires reconsideration of established knowledge production alike'.[7] Furthermore, community-based archives enable community groups to determine the contents of the repositories as needed and decided upon by their community.[8] This can also signify control over the access to and use of materials. With growing interest in ID-SOV and ID-GOV, Indigenous people can initiate, develop and engage with community archives on their own terms, which is essential to facilitate self-determination.[9] By applying community archiving techniques, the desire to create histories that represent the experiences of everyday marginalised people and groups makes hidden narratives visible.[10] For example, repositories created by mainstream archives (e.g., galleries, libraries or universities, etc.) in partnership with ICAs are a means by which Indigenous communities can create and maintain archival systems that are inclusive and respectful of Aboriginal and Torres Strait Islander protocols and needs.[11] This article refers to ICAs as information and knowledge repositories that contain records of significance to Indigenous community groups.

Indigenous data governance

ID-SOV and ID-GOV are part of a growing global movement and associated research that has emerged in response to poor and unjust data practices concerning the control, creation, collection and access to Indigenous knowledge.[12] ID-SOV refers to the rights of Indigenous people to determine 'the collection, use, and application of data about us, our lands, and cultures',[13] whilst ID-GOV refers to the ownership, access, generation and management of Indigenous data by Indigenous people and nations.[14]

ID-SOV is achieved through the exercise of ID-GOV.[15] Indigenous communities practice ID-SOV through the interconnected processes of ID-GOV and data decolonisation.[16] Decolonisation occurs through exposing, challenging and transforming the dominant hegemonic norms and values in data collection and management.[17] This enables Indigenous communities and other data representatives to replace and repurpose Western data systems with Indigenous frameworks and knowledge that 'define data and inform how it is collected and used'.[18] In this way, ID-GOV is informed by Indigenous ontology and epistemology, or Indigenous ways of knowing, doing and being, to control and manage community data practices.[19]

The practice of ID-GOV is encapsulated in the CARE Principles (Collective benefit, Authority to control, Responsibility and Ethics) developed with the support of the Global Indigenous Data Alliance (GIDA).[20] These principles emerged from the efforts of 'Te Mana Raraunga Maori Data Sovereignty Network, US Indigenous Data Sovereignty (ID-SOV) Network, Maiam Nayri Wingara Aboriginal and Torres Strait Islander Data Sovereignty Collective, and numerous Indigenous people, nations, and communities'.[21] The CARE principles aim to ensure that through ID-GOV First Nations, people are no longer alienated from the collection, management and use of Indigenous data. However, the extent to which Indigenous groups partake in the four processes varies globally.

Currently, four ID-SOV networks exist internationally: the First Nations Information Governance Centre (FNIGC) in operation in Canada since 2010; Te Mana Raraunga, The Mâori Data Sovereignty launched in 2015; the United States Indigenous Data Sovereignty Network formed in 2016; and Maiam Nayri Wingara Aboriginal and Torres Strait Islander Data Sovereignty Collective established in Australia in 2017.[22] Following the Oñati workshop in July, GIDA was launched with contributions from the cofounders of these ID-SOV networks.[23] Importantly, GIDA considers that 'global alliance is needed to advocate and advance a shared vision for ID-SOV' (GIDA 2021) as UNDRIP alone is not sufficient to achieve this (for further details, see the 2019 Oñati Indigenous Data Sovereignty Communique).[24]

In Australia, there is growing interest and advocacy to progress ID-SOV and ID-GOV. For example, in 2017, Maiam Nayri Wingara was initiated by Indigenous scholars to promote shared understandings and the development of Aboriginal and Torres Strait Islander data sovereignty principles and protocols.[25] Guided by UNDRIP, Maiam Nayri Wingara actively encourages Indigenous Australians to engage in the data space using Australian ID-GOV protocols and principles to empower communities to accurately record their stories. The National Centre for Indigenous Genomics (NCIG), based at the Australian National University, exemplifies the progression of ID-SOV and ID-GOV in the Australian context. It was established in 2013 to house a vast collection of DNA blood samples of First Nations people from across Australia.[26] With Indigenous-led decision-making and management of the data, NCIG utilises genomic medicine to the benefit of First Nations Australians.[27] It is evident, therefore, that ID-GOV enables Aboriginal and Torres Strait Islander peoples to make appropriate decisions that support local Indigenous communities to meet their needs and aspirations, especially in sustaining community archives.[28]

Research methodology

A case study approach was adopted to investigate the unique circumstances of the KRIC Archives. The value of using a case study approach lies in its insightful appreciation of the context and other complex conditions related to a given situation or 'case' through its use of multiple sources of evidence.[29] In this way, it fits well with an Indigenous research paradigm, in which it can readily encompass Indigenous beliefs and ways of being.[30] Understanding the ways in which Aboriginal and Torres Strait Islander people make sense of the world, especially the complex connection between life, land and the cosmos, is a crucial component of Indigenous research.[31] Indigenous worldviews differ greatly from 'the dominant cultural worldview in Western society' and consequently are often excluded from the Western research frameworks.[32] Even when Indigenous knowledge is acknowledged, it is often from a Eurocentric standpoint.[33] An Indigenous paradigm and research methodology, however, allow First Nations communities (and researchers) to '(re)present our worldviews from the basis from which we live, learn and survive' and reclaim control over Indigenous knowledge.[34] Therefore, as a Torres Strait Islander researcher, I adopted Indigenous research methodology, first to give precedence to Indigenous frameworks and ways of knowing, being and doing. Second, to ensure that power in the research relationship is transferred from the researcher to the researched by advocating Aboriginal and Torres Strait Islander community agendas and interests.[35] Considering the Traditional Owners on whose land this research was conducted, I aimed to systematically investigate the perspectives and opinions of the Aboriginal and other First Nations people living in the north-eastern region of Victoria. In doing so, I consulted with Kaiela Institute and their Algabonyah Data, Research and Evaluation Unit (ADREU) and obtained approval via an application process to conduct the study in a culturally safe manner.

In keeping with the case study approach, I used a combination of data collection methods to ensure a range of different types of research data.[36] They included a small number of semi-structured in-depth interviews, archival material sourced from the KRIC Archives and my autoethnographic reflections. These methods ensured both Indigenous and Western knowledge were specifically investigated to generate a better understanding of KRIC's data practices.[37]

The research data were analysed thematically using a colour coding system. By this means a specific colour was assigned to each and every theme identified in the interview, archival and autoethnographic data. The data were then analysed using the colour codes to identify recurring themes. The synthesis of the data in this way enabled its interpretation as it presented insights and understanding of the ways KRIC realised ID-GOV.

Semi-structured interviews
Using convenience sampling, study participants were identified and recruited from a sample population of individuals involved in the KRIC Archives, either as part of the KRIC Archiving Project team or through the KRIC office. Semi-structured, in-depth interviews were conducted with each individual and guided by a set list of questions that asked participants to reflect on their own personal experience with KRIC and working in the KRIC Archives. The questions also inquired into the ways in which the Archives were meaningful to each participant, the significance of the Archives to the community and the participant's familiarity with the concept of ID-GOV.

The interviewees comprised four of the original 10 members of the Archiving Project team employed in the KRIC Archives from 2006 to 2015. Each participant was given a project information statement sheet outlining the research project. It invited them to participate in an interview and advised them that all information collected would be treated anonymously and confidentially. Once they consented to being interviewed, participants were asked to sign a consent form prior to the interviews taking place. All interviews were digitally recorded using a voice recorder, transcribed with the assistance of transcription software and analysed thematically.

Analysis of archiving protocol and practices
In addition to interviews, materials held within the KRIC Archives were used as a secondary data set. Documents pertaining to archiving policies and practices of the KRIC Archiving Project were examined as evidence for determining whether and how the Project was realising ID-GOV. Documents such as meeting minutes, Memorandum of Understandings (MoUs), and archival policies and practices formed part of the data that were analysed for the research. Access to and use of archival data were approved under an ID-GOV framework developed by the ADREU at Kaiela Institute, the current location of the KRIC Archives.

Autoethnographic reflection

My positionality and reflexivity as an insider researcher are embedded in the study through the process of autoethnographic reflection. I consider and refer to myself as an 'insider' on two fronts, both as an Indigenous person living in the community under consideration and as a former member of the KRIC Archiving Project team. By locating myself within the context of the KRIC Archives, I situate my own positionality and reflexivity within the research, by which I can 'fulfil cultural, ethical and relational obligations; and recentre [Indigenous] axiology and ontology'.[38] My personal account constitutes part of the data gathered for this case study and further centres Indigenous ways of being, doing and knowing within the research.[39] Accordingly, I actively disengage from deficit discourses through employing a narrative of strength, resilience and self-determination. By adopting a strength-based perspective and language, the research aimed to take into account the community's sustained efforts to improve economic, social and health outcomes for First Nations Australians through self-determined data governance.

The KRIC office and archives

The KRIC office was established in 1988 and became a hub for Indigenous community activity in the Goulburn Murray region in northern Victoria.[40] It supported an array of Indigenous organisations, groups and programs through the development of capacity building initiatives.[41] These aimed to support community development, cross-cultural awareness and public discussion.[42]

I recall that the 'White House' – as it was affectionately referred to by locals – was as the name implied, a small white house set against the neighbouring cookie cutter shopfronts. Whilst the facade was like that of a domestic residence, internally, KRIC resembled a functional office space: bedrooms as offices, the dining and living area as meeting spaces, and the backrooms converted to storage and printing areas. Like many organisations, as the activities within the KRIC offices grew or changed, so did the functional spaces within the White House.

The KRIC Archives were and remain directly connected to the organisational activity of the KRIC office, as most of the records were produced or received at the KRIC office, by KRIC or by the various Indigenous organisations that operated there before winding up or relocating to separate premises. For this reason, the Archives were able to grow organically from the late 1980s.[43] In his work on the history of the Victorian Aboriginal Advancement League, Broome emphasises that Indigenous people express self-determination and agency by using colonial systems and concepts to forge better pathways for themselves.[44] The changing political, social and economic agendas of elected governments and the development of community organisations, groups and programs are evident in the complexity of the KRIC Archives. In this way, much can be learnt about the local Indigenous history through the KRIC Archives as the various sections of the collection provide a series of narratives, conversations and aspirations of the community in those moments. The type of community initiatives whose activities contribute to these narratives includes sports, health, education, employment and financial literacy (to name a few). Whilst each Indigenous community organisation has its own purpose and course of action, its role within the larger narrative of the Indigenous community's survival and growth is connected to other activities captured by the Archives. Thus, it is not just about the history of any one organisation or group but reflects a collective purpose and drive for self-determination.

The KRIC archiving project

KRIC formed two notable partnerships with local organisations to develop the KRIC Archives. These were the Goulburn Valley Regional Library (GVRL) and the Aboriginal Community Strategic Planning and Policy Unit (ACSPPU). The ACSPPU was a resource for the

Indigenous community to undertake a range of community development processes. It was also a resource for local Aboriginal leadership in providing policy and planning support but is no longer in operation as it amalgamated with KRIC in 2011 to become the Kaiela Institute.[45]

Memoranda of understanding signed between KRIC and these organisations demonstrated mutually beneficial relationships. The ACSPPU was interested in housing the non-active portion of the KRIC Archives due to the wealth of information about past and present programs contained within the collection.[46] KRIC, on the other hand, needed more storage space for its expanding collection. The relationship between the GVRL and KRIC aimed to develop a partnership that would nurture a repository of 'Indigenous information and knowledge that would be accessible and responsive to the needs of the local community'.[47] The Koori Library Pathways Project as it was termed sought to connect Indigenous and non-Indigenous people to the Indigenous culture, history and heritage of the Goulburn Murray region. It was from this partnership that the KRIC Archiving Project came to fruition. A small number of Indigenous community members, including myself, were employed to sort, catalogue and index KRIC's accumulating records. This small group was known as the KRIC Archiving Project team. Such partnerships show the resourcefulness of KRIC and the Indigenous community in utilising other organisations to overcome limitations in the development of the Archives.

The KRIC Archiving Project attained a contextual review of its collection, known as a significance assessment, in 2009.[48] The review used research into the activities of KRIC and other local Indigenous organisations and the evaluation of other Indigenous archives (in contrast to the KRIC Archives) to determine the historical, aesthetic, scientific and social/spiritual values of the KRIC Archives.[49] The purpose of the assessment was to appraise the value and meaning of the material within the collection to provide a basis upon which decisions about its management could be made. The Significance Assessment provided several recommendations for the ongoing development and management of the Archives. These included the continued sorting and indexing of archival material, establishing a cataloguing system, developing links with research institutions, investigating access issues, seeking further funding, recruiting volunteers, exhibiting archival material, raising community awareness, and continued assistance for the survivors and descendants of the Stolen Generations in accessing the collection.[50]

Due to the changing nature of Indigenous affairs, KRIC was re-named as the Kaiela Institute in 2011.[51] During the process, the Archives were relocated on several occasions, and as a result, it became disorganised. Furthermore, a lack of funding support meant the continued indexing and sorting of materials ceased in 2015, and the Archives in their current state remain incomplete and dormant.

The connection between the activity of the KRIC office and the KRIC Archives not only is an important component of understanding the local Indigenous history but also demonstrates the community's efforts towards achieving self-determination by representing a counter narrative to frameworks of white hegemony. This narrative repositions the value of First Nations people from a deficit to a strength-based discourse. Recognising the importance of the collection prompted a partnership between GVRL and KRIC, from which eventuated the KRIC Archiving Project. It was there, in 2008, that I first came to work on the Archives as a member of the KRIC Archiving Project team.

Interview and autoethnographic findings

The four participants interviewed for the research were all members of the local and surrounding communities of Shepparton who had either grown up in the area or who had resided there for many years. All had experience working across mainstream and Indigenous organisations in both the private and public sectors. Participants came to work on the KRIC

Archives through various means, including hearing about the project via word-of-mouth within the local Indigenous community, followed by a successful interview for a position. Others were already employed at KRIC in different capacities or were introduced through other community and organisational partnerships with KRIC and/or the Archiving Project. As a member of the archiving team, I was also a resident of the Shepparton area and member of the local Indigenous community and was recruited to the Archiving Project through an interview process.

Origin of the KRIC archiving project
The first theme to emerge from the data analysis of the interviews was in regard to the origins of the KRIC Archiving Project. Interviewees identified the Project as arising from the need to organise and preserve the personal collection of various materials belonging to an Indigenous community leader, who had initiated and lead many local and regional activities and organisations. Such organisations and activities included KRIC, the Rumbalara Football Netball Club (RFNC), one of two Indigenous owned and operated football clubs in Victoria and is deeply rooted in the histories of the Yorta Yorta and the football teams of Cummeragunja Reserve in New South Wales.[52] The Academy of Sports Health and Education (ASHE) is a regional, Indigenous focused, sports health and education centre and was developed almost two decades ago by the RFNC in partnership with the University of Melbourne Department of Rural Health, Shepparton in 2004.[53]

The records from this personal collection formed the basis of the KRIC Archives. As one participant commented, in referring to the personal origins of the archival collection, '… it was really [the community leader's] own, in many ways … [their] own information …' (Interviewee 3). Several others explained how these records had been systematically accumulated by the community leader over time.

> … that's how part of it come about. Because of [the community leader] having all this information from all these different committees and things that were just in the back of [their] car … or in [their] shed that needed to be documented and, you know, filed away for future use (Interviewee 4).

> … that's kind of the start, because … someone would say, 'Oh, you need to clean your car, you know. You need to throw those papers out' and [the community leader] never would. And [they] would always collect them and pile them together and then put them in [their] [car] boot … (Interviewee 2).

The sheer volume of records resulted in community interest to organise these records and successful efforts to secure funding from various sources to archive them. This is highlighted in the following quote:

> And then, you know, we got to a point where it was just like, 'Wow, we just got too much paper! [LAUGHS] … So, we're gonna have to do something with it …' And they applied for this Koori Library Pathways Project funding, and we were able to use a little bit of that. And then somewhere, I think, along the line, we actually got funded for it … And then we got a little bit more money. And that's when we were able to get a few more people on to go through and actually build this archiving project … So, we were able to build a little team, purely for this cause … (Interviewee 2).

In my own experience, identifying the origin of the Archives was key to realising the complex interconnections between the documents and the community development work of [the community leader]. It was one of the first things that I learnt as part of the Archiving Project team, and it gave me a better comprehension of the sorting and filing process; I better understood why a document was organised within a specific volume and series.

Meaning and importance of the KRIC archives

The need to preserve the rich source of information and knowledge accumulating in the community leader's personal collection was reinforced once work began on the Archiving Project. The tasks of sorting and reading documents not only highlighted the importance of making the material accessible but also presented the archive workers an opportunity to learn from the past and reaffirm their heritage and identity. For example, in response to the question, 'In what ways are the KRIC Archives meaningful to you?', one team member responded,

> ... radical, firstly because it was that paper trail ... a historical perspective on the contribution we're making to, not only Shepparton, but Victoria and to the nation. And that alone is hugely important because that's a new approach to what we do. Keeping the documents, I mean the paper trail, it's totally new ... (Interviewee 1).

In this participant's view, the Archives, '... gives a really good perspective of the Indigenous philosophy around how everything is related to everything else ...' (Interviewee 1). The connections between individual, family, community and their intersection across place and time were encapsulated for them within the KRIC Archives. The importance of the records extended beyond physical symbolism, by maintaining the spiritual principles of connectedness particularly how everything is interrelated,

> You have Aboriginal studies, but you don't have philosophies. The Archives actually has that and it's all in paper form and it is set up in ways where, if you're Indig [sic], you can see how they connect, one to the other (Interviewee 1).

In my experience, the spiritual symbolism of the Archives was particularly remarkable. The interconnections between archival material; community activities, organisations, groups and programs; and their narrative as a collective were indicative of 'one-ness'. It embodied the ongoing interrelatedness between land and people, living and non-living, and the past and the present, and it enabled me to appreciate how I am a part of that as an Indigenous person.

Memories and significance of the KRIC Archives

The memories of working in the KRIC Archives recalled by the interviewees were positive. For example, one participant explained how history was reclaimed through joyful discoveries in the Archives, '... we had these really beautiful kind of moments through it ...' (Interviewee 2). They also valued the significance of such discoveries 'it was those little precious moments with people as they were discovering what we were all learning' (Interviewee 2). Similarly, for another interviewee, the legacy was recognised when processing audio material,

> ... a lot of the people [recorded] on the CDs would now be Elders because they were mostly music or interviews done of young people by young people at the time and those young people would have families now ... (Interviewee 1).

The social impact of the KRIC Archives for interviewees accords with the findings of Caswell and colleagues.[54] Their study of the impacts of community-driven archives on the people and communities they serve in California demonstrates how the significance of discovering family, friends and neighbours in archival materials fosters and strengthens connection to community.⁵⁵ This impact also encouraged a level of pride amongst the interviewees towards the history and activity of the local Indigenous community, 'it's a very progressive community, the Yorta Yorta one is, the fastest growing and most politically astute community, not only in Victoria, but all in Australia' (Interviewee 1). The Archives maintained and preserved the narratives, diligence and contributions of community and its Elders benefitting future generations,

> ... it's good to know what you've been doing ... if someone like yourself wants to do a history of ... Aboriginal community in Shepparton, well it's good to see those different ventures (Interviewee 3).

This passing on of knowledge through the Archives was seen as significant in safeguarding against loss of community history held orally by community knowledge holders '... an Elder who has all these wonderful stories they keep to themselves and when they die, they're lost ...' (Interviewee 4). I, myself, recall a specific moment when the Archiving Project was attempting to identify individuals from an old black and white photo of a local football team. We asked aunties and uncles, most of whom had just dropped into the White House, if they could help identify the individuals in the photo. In this way, we were able to identify many of the past players and rekindle community memories and history in the process.

For participants, the Archives were 'a little goldmine' (Interviewee 2), and working on the Project was 'a stroke of luck ...' (Interviewee 3). This accords with my own impression of the Archives as a unique repository of knowledge, and hence, the inspiration behind this research. Recognition of the exceptional nature of the Archives was further evident amongst the interviewees by their use of terms such as 'standalone' (Interviewee 1), 'pushing the way' (Interviewee 2) and 'breaking new ground' (Interviewee 4).

Challenges with the KRIC archiving project

Challenges regarding the short- and long-term sustainability of the Archives were a concern for the participants. As one explained, weekly team meetings provided ongoing evaluation of the indexing system,

> ... once a week or once every two weeks we would go through the system and [the coordinator] would get everyone to talk about whether it was working, or not working or if they were having problems with it. And I think that's how we ironed it out ... (Interviewee 1).

The absence of a data management framework, combined with the vastness of the work and lack of knowledge about the content of the Archives, however, required trusting those who worked on the KRIC Archives to engage with the material in an appropriate manner. As a result, the task of refining the indexing system became 'too complex in the end' (Interviewee 2).

During the archiving process, several factors were identified as necessary for the sustainability and development of the Archives,

> ... we said that it was really important for people to show proof of ID when they want[ed] to access the Archives. The other thing we needed to get was a reading room (Interviewee 1).

A reading room for users and proof of their identity were essential not only for the ease of community access but also for the overall security of the archival material. Participants also found it a challenge to simultaneously protect the materials and make them accessible to the community without having specialised skills.

I think in the first instance, yes, we wanted it to be accessible to community, but I think we were trying to do other things first. So, one, we had to protect the document and then two, we had to kind of make it accessible, even just to ourselves ... And I don't think we quite had the skill set amongst ourselves to manage how ... community could utilise it (Interviewee 2).

Notably, members of the KRIC Archiving Project utilised training opportunities from mainstream institutions to advance the Archives' protocols and procedures. Workshops through the National Library, the National Film and Sound Archive, the National Archives and Public Records of Victoria 'trained us into how all of those collection agencies do their Archives ...' and '... we met up with other collection agencies all around Australia' (Interviewee 1). As such, interviewees emphasised the difficulty of managing access and security of the Archives, which, on occasion, was underappreciated by other team members and staff who had not undertaken the training workshops. Interviewee 1 explained that '... with the Archives we had a process, so that was something that we'd learnt at the workshops in Canberra ...' and

... even though we did great work, it was really difficult for everyone else to appreciate how hard it was to put it together and to follow those security measures. Because during that time a couple of documents out went missing, but we also relocated [the Archives] like three or four times (Interviewee 1).

Interviewee 4 added,

... have a little bit of ... some guidelines about ... accessing that information and what you can do with it and what you can't do with it, so people can access it, but it's not open access where it can be used for unscrupulous things ... (Interviewee 4).

It was also important to participants to have the collection digitised, '... you've still got an opportunity to possibly digitise it ...' (Interviewee 3). Digitised records prevented any further deterioration to the Archives and eased access by making copies available electronically.[56]

The variety of archival material and lack of specialised skills meant that the KRIC Archiving Project was limited to coding and cataloguing certain data whilst continuing to adapt existing archiving protocols. This was required as the indexing system had not yet been developed to include all the archival materials. The Project was also constrained by funding and the costs associated with access to appropriate equipment and implementing certain processes. As participants stated '... we didn't have the money to keep going ...' (Interviewee 1) and,

... we're talking about keeping things, you know, with acid paper, and all that kind of stuff. We never ever got to that point, but we were talking about digital, but we don't quite have the programs that we do today ... it'd be different to do it nowadays, but we were just learning (Interviewee 2).

These findings regarding access to resources, limited funding and issues with developing archival protocols echo those of Zavala and colleagues who observed similar challenges and concern with the long- and short-term sustainability of community archives in Southern California.[57]

Use of the KRIC archiving project colour coding system

According to the interviewees, KRIC developed its own archiving protocols and guidelines through the support of the GVRL. Descriptions of the archival systems included the categorising of material according to local institutions; type of activity; dates; and the use of plastic pockets, coloured folders and dots. As one interviewee recalled,

> I know we went by year, and I know we categorised by organisation … that's how [Name of Manager] started to see that map because we knew what organisations we were dealing with and what organisations [community leader] had been working across and then … We broke it down by the year. And … then by the date of the document, if it had a date. And all the documents that were, didn't have a date. So, date unknown, kind of, were at the front … I think we tried to kind of file it like that … We had colour, so we colour coded by folder. The folders were the colours. So, because I remember the [football] Club being orange, I'm pretty sure and then ATSIC, I think was blue and yeah. So, I'm pretty sure we had kind of that. I can't remember what the dots were for, I know, I know we put the dots on the plastic slips … And they were to do something, and I can't quite remember what they were … (Interviewee 2).

The development of a mud map by the Archiving Project Coordinator outlined the interconnection between community organisations, and community initiatives assisted Archiving members in refining the sorting and filing process. Following this, a colour coding system was incorporated, although it was a less significant component of the archival system. As one interviewee recalled, 'colour coding came much later. I think, just before we had the significance assessment done' (Interviewee 1). Another stated, 'I can't remember, I just remember that there was a colour coding system' (Interviewee 2). Similarly, in my own experience, I can recall aspects of a colour coding system, however, I cannot remember having ever used the system.

Perceived community significance of the KRIC Archives

Community interest in the Archives was apparent, particularly in the documentation of organisational activity and community history, which was an important resource both internally to KRIC staff and externally to community and universities. As Interviewee 1 explained, 'it was community who walked in off the street and asked if they could use stuff. It was University students ringing up and saying can they access stuff'. However, it was later identified that stricter guidelines were required to make the Archives accessible in a culturally safe manner to community. Another interviewee commented,

> you know, there's privacy, confidentiality, there's things that you know …, you want to protect but at the same time you want to make it accessible …, that set balance … that's why you need those guidelines (Interviewee 3).

Understanding ID-GOV

The KRIC Archives were recognised as determining '… the rules and frameworks around how data is managed and looked after' (Interviewee 2). Whilst not all participants had a prior understanding of ID-GOV, once I explained the concept to them using a standardised definition, they immediately related ID-GOV to the KRIC Archives.[58] For example, one commented, 'that is the KRIC Archives all over, it does all of that stuff' (Interviewee 1). Interestingly, interviewees also expressed an understanding of ID-SOV when discussing the community's ownership and control of the KRIC archival material. The Archives were seen as containing material, which went well beyond quantitative data. They also included text which could be analysed to provide evidence and build history, you could get all that kind of stuff that text, kind of discourse via the documents, they're creating, you know, about themselves. And that becomes evidence of their legacy or their organisational legacy, you know, what a history, build their history, a whole heap of things. And so yeah, for me, I think, they own it, it's their archive. So, it's community owned already. It's not a database that the government owns, and we have to get permission to access (Interviewee 2).

A common concern for the interviewees was community decision-making and guidance regarding the use of data to ensure that it was for the benefit of all and not just individual researchers,

> … communities being able to guide you in the best way that that data should be used for the benefit of all … At the moment, it's very one-sided, you know, and only the researcher really benefits, and the community just gets left … (Interviewee 2).

> … a lot of non-indigenous researchers go in, collect the information and there's no, in the past, no real acknowledgement of ownership. The ownership becomes the University and not the community (Interviewee 4).

Perceptions of KRIC as an expression of self-determination and/or decolonisation

When discussing how non-Indigenous volunteers visited the KRIC office during their un-rostered time or days off, Interviewee 1 stated, '… they'd say, "but I just like it here. I just want to come in and have a cuppa" or you know come in and say hello …'. Interviewee 3 reiterated this sentiment, '… KRIC, was very friendly …'. Their experience of working in the KRIC Archiving Project and the KRIC office in general accords with my own memory of KRIC as a workplace unlike any other I had experienced before. It seamlessly integrated both Indigenous and mainstream practices in a way that was comfortable for all who worked or visited there. Others described it as a community space and '… kind of this little community hub and support …' (Interviewee 2). KRIC was a place where,

> … Community could pop in make a cuppa, we'd all make, share our lunch, throw in and buy food and if anyone walked in off the street, they were welcome to have a feed … (Interviewee 4).

Additionally, several interviewees found the working culture at KRIC to be a 'freer atmosphere' compared to their experiences of working in the more formal settings of mainstream and other Indigenous organisations. As a result, they valued KRIC as an ideal work environment. For example, one explained,

> … as a work environment, for me it was perfect cause it meant that I could work at whatever speed I wanted to and pick the times that I would work as well …. You've got no one looking over your shoulder, and you've got no one watching the clock to make sure that you're meeting milestones … And you've pretty much got a lot of freedom to do the work when you think it's the best time to go and do it (Interviewee 1).

Here, the flexibility of Indigenous organisations juxtaposed the rigidity of mainstream government and corporate structures. KRIC was able to meld Indigenous knowledge systems and practices with Western institutional frameworks and understandings. As Interviewee 1 highlighted, '… you've got two ends of the one world there, working in the one space'.

The KRIC Archives were also seen as a testament to the self-determination of the Yorta Yorta people. For example,

> ... community here is not, they're not passive, they're not passive to their own disadvantage, they *have* been doing things, and that is evidence of that, that they have been active in this space. And that they have achieved a lot, you know, via their activity and leadership and hard work and whatever. And that's, as a collection, that's what it tells you, you know ... If you join up all the Archives of all organizations here, you could just imagine what you've got. It's a massive amount of activity that this community is doing for themselves, you know, they're not just sitting there going, 'Oh, here, I want a handout', they're actually helping themselves (Interviewee 2).

> ... it's a reflection of their communities and you, and your own sense of looking after yourselves. You cannot ... rely on other people to do it. So, it's best to do it yourself ... (Interviewee 3).

> it's history, it's past history, it's ... documents. You know, a lot of work had been done in the eighties, a lot of good work ... A lot of things documented about where we're at in the eighties, what our issues were and what we were trying to do to overcome some of those issues. So, it's all there in the Archives (Interviewee 4).

Analysis of the KRIC archiving project's policies and practices

The KRIC Archiving Project team developed a number of policy and procedure documents, which incorporated data management standards for identifying and organising materials within the KRIC Archives.[59] The documents informed how archival material was being managed by community. One example of adapting Western archival standards was the Project's use of the Public Records Office of Victoria's publication on the storage of public records in agencies.[60] This utilisation of technical information regarding the storage, maintenance and disposal of data illustrates KRIC's data governance model.[61] The model had distinct sections into which archival material was sorted and demonstrates the community's plans for continued maintenance of the collection.

Two distinct filing systems operated under the indexing guidelines as KRIC's 'current active material' required a filing process separate from the archiving system. Current material would eventually circulate into the archiving system after 2 years. Once material had been sorted, indexed and filed, it was then stored in allocated rooms within the KRIC office or the ACSPPU office. Certain rooms housed specific series. For example, general material was stored in 'Room 1' at the ACSPPU, whilst books and publications were stored in 'Room 2' at the KRIC office, and private and confidential material housed in 'Room 3' at the KRIC office. Such efforts are evidence of the community's attempts to adapt mainstream archival standards to suit the framework of their circumstances and work within the limits of their organisational environment. Whilst initially incorporating only two series (i.e., 'General' and 'Books & Publications'), the index was eventually expanded to eight series and spread across six rooms due to the large volume of archival material.

Further to the indexing and storage of archival material was a colour coding system. The system worked in parallel with the other indexing standards. Coloured paper dot stickers were attached to shelf lists for easier identification of archival material by the KRIC staff permitted to access the Archives at that time. The colour coding system specifically incorporated the epistemology and ontology of Indigenous culture. This was evident in the complex way colour was used to connect each category. For example, an outer green ring and yellow centre referred to the 'Missions/Reserves' category, whereas an outer yellow ring and green centre represented 'Song and Dance'. However, both green and yellow were also connected to other colours and other classifications within the system. For instance, an outer yellow ring and blue centre referred to the 'Arts & Material Cultures' set, whilst an outer green ring and pink centre belonged to the 'Flora/Fauna' category.

Findings and discussion
The KRIC Archiving Project clearly challenged the exclusionary framework of Western archival science for Indigenous communities. This was achieved by centring the voices of Aboriginal and Torres Strait Islander people within the framework of KRIC's archival practices. By recognising the continuation of social injustice arising from structural forces which marginalise and overlook such voices, the Archiving Project was able to temporarily ameliorate the impacts of Western institutional structures and policies in the operation and management of the KRIC Archives. Achieving such outcomes was possible through the connection and collaboration of the Indigenous and mainstream domains.

The KRIC office functioned as a cultural interface between the Indigenous and mainstream community, in which it provided a socially inclusive and comfortable space connected to and supportive of Indigenous and non-Indigenous people.[62] By establishing common ground, KRIC advocated the needs of Indigenous people through its community development work whilst satisfying funding requirements of government policies for Aboriginal affairs. Furthermore, community leadership and innovation allowed KRIC to manage, decipher and transform relationships between the Indigenous community and mainstream agencies, with limited resources and support that such a task required.[63] In bridging both worlds, KRIC fostered a unique organisational culture.

The accommodating and culturally attuned organisational culture at KRIC expressed the characteristics of an Indigenous work ethic. This contrasts with the neo-liberal capitalist work ethic driven by rational calculation, efficiency and profit-making, which obligates employees to perform, manage and complete tasks within strict timeframes.[64] Whilst KRIC staff were still required to meet performance standards and management outcomes through their successful completion of tasks, such outcomes were achieved through a more relaxed and inclusive approach. It is important to note that whilst examining this Indigenous work ethic was beyond the scope of this research, it did—along with collaborative practices—contribute to successful outcomes. This explicit expression of Indigenous knowledge and culture was at the core of KRIC's organisational structure and purpose. It was also a milieu of community agency, self-determination, innovation and cultural affirmation that incubated the KRIC Archives. The Archives, as a result, did not emerge as a 'troubling space'[65] that many mainstream information repositories, such as colonial archives, can present for Indigenous people.

KRIC's organisational culture and the work performed in that space reiterated a need to find a sustainable solution to accruing data. The procurement of small grants assisted with establishing an archiving project to deal with the accumulating material. Through the funding grants, KRIC was able to employ a small, dedicated team to focus on the sorting and filing of the collection. Noticeably, the Archives developed and provided a much-needed physical record that enabled the continued efforts of the Indigenous community to preserve, manage, control and make decisions regarding their history. As a community archive, KRIC's close affinity with its records meant it could accommodate the voices and visions of community to evolve archival thinking.[66] It was also a medium through which community could create new ways of connecting across time and space.

The KRIC Archives empower community narratives and histories and, thus, convey the living memory, epistemology and ontology of Yorta Yorta Nations people.[67] Therefore, rather than being something inherently Western, the KRIC Archives privilege Indigenous oral traditions transmitted through records.[68] Here, the continuum of Yorta Yorta history and knowledge, which has passed from one generation to the next for millennia, is embodied in the KRIC Archives.

The relationships that exist between Indigenous people and records, and the complexities that surround those connections impact the individuals whose histories the KRIC Archives document. Additionally, the individuals, communities and organisations who share in the vision of the Archives enriched and broadened their recordkeeping and archival practices.[69] This is evident in the various narratives captured within the archival material that reveal the extensive and dynamic activity by community to challenge colonial discourse. In this context, the KRIC Archiving Project is evidence of the Yorta Yorta Nations' self-determination and decolonisation of public collecting institutions. By adapting the typical Western archival frameworks to suit the unique circumstances of the Archives and challenging deeper social justice issues, KRIC created an appropriate archival framework for the Aboriginal and other First Nations community. Through the coding and cataloguing process, the KRIC Archiving Project formed a culture of inquiry to question, learn, understand and transform the standard Western archival practices and protocols. The collective ownership, control, creation, access and preservation of Indigenous data demonstrate KRIC's approach to data governance.[70] KRIC realised ID-GOV by integrating Indigenous ways of knowing, doing and being in the control and management of their archival data practices.[71] As such, the community's agency, self-determination and shared vision drove KRIC's data governance model.

Although the KRIC Archiving Project had developed a functional Indigenous-led data governance model, the lack of ongoing funding meant that this emergence of ID-GOV could not be sustained. Community archives have precarious futures, in which they operate predominantly through their ability to access and retain resources such as 'financial, human, physical, skills and expertise'.[72] The short-term and long-term sustainability of the KRIC Archives relied on similar resources. Its longevity was particularly vulnerable to a precarious funding situation, lack of knowledge and skills in archival science and the vastness of materials which eventually saw the Archives and the activities of the Archiving Project cease. This is not to say that the KRIC Archives no longer exist, but rather, they lie dormant awaiting revival and the activation of the Significance Assessment recommendations.

Conclusion

ICAs are a testament to Aboriginal and Torres Strait Islander interest in controlling, preserving, collecting and accessing Indigenous knowledge and history. In this regard, the KRIC Archives were and continue to be a significant and very valuable resource, particularly as the Archives and the Archiving Project reflect the cultural heritage, identity and pride of the Yorta Yorta community; document the efforts of community to maintain their data rights and rights of self-determination across changing times; and represent a counter narrative to Western archival practices. However, the range of materials in the Archives, its precarious funding situation and the lack of archival knowledge and skills needed to maintain the Archives over time have resulted in it becoming dormant. This research concludes, therefore, that the KRIC Archives challenged the rigidity of institutional frameworks through what was a momentary realisation of ID-GOV.

The research findings demonstrate that funding and training opportunities are essential for the long-term sustainability of Indigenous archives and ID-GOV. Also, it is necessary that the decolonisation of archival institutional systems and processes employs more inclusive and collaborative practices for and with marginalised communities. Given that this research is a single case study, an important question that arises is whether and how other ICAs utilise similar data governance models that challenge Western archival practices. Therefore, further research investigating data governance models developed by ICAs elsewhere is needed to demonstrate the direct effects on their respective communities and their significance and value to them.

Disclosure statement
No potential conflict of interest was reported by the author.

Data availability statement
The data that support the findings of this study are available on request from the corresponding author. The data are not publicly available due to their containing information that could compromise the privacy of research participants. Non-digital data supporting this study are curated at the Kaiela Institute Inc, Shepparton, Victoria.

Acknowledgements
I wish to acknowledge the traditional custodians on whose land this research was conducted, the Yorta Yorta Nation, and pay my respect to Elders, past, present and emerging. I would like to express my appreciation to Dr. Lucinda Aberdeen for her invaluable feedback and guidance throughout this process, and whose input improved this manuscript significantly. Special thanks to my sister, Dr. Tui Crumpen, for sharing her wisdom and without whom this research would be uninspired. I would also like to thank Paul Briggs OAM, the research participants and the Kaiela Institute for their support of this study.

Notes

1. Shannon Faulkhead, 'Connecting through Records: Narratives of Koorie Victoria', Archives and Manuscripts, vol. 37, no. 2, 2009, pp. 60–88.
2. Shani Crumpen, 'Realising Indigenous Data Governance: A Case Study of the Koori Resource and Information Centre Archives', BA Honours dissertation, La Trobe University, 2021.
3. Sarah Baker and Zelmarie Cantillon, 'Safeguarding Australia's Community Heritage Sector: A Consideration of the Institutional Wellbeing of Volunteer-Managed Galleries, Libraries, Archives, Museums and Historical Societies', Australian Historical Studies, vol. 5, no. 1, 2020, p. 71. doi: 10.1080/1031461X.2019.1659836
4. Rebecka Sheffield, 'Community Archives', in Heather MacNeil and Terry Eastwood (eds.), Currents of Archival Thinking, Libraries Unlimited, Exeter, UK, 2017, p. 352.
5. Kirsten Thorpe, 'Aboriginal Community Archives', in Anne Gilliland, Sue McKemmish and Andrew Lau (eds.), Archival Multiverse, Monash University Press, Clayton, VIC, 2017, p. 903; See also Andrew Flinn, 'Community Histories, Community Archives: Some Opportunities and Challenges', Journal of the Society of Archivists, vol. 28, no. 2, 2007, pp. 151–176. doi: 10.1080/00379810701611936
6. Leisa Gibbons, 'Community Archives in Australia: A Preliminary Investigation', Journal of the Australian Library and Information Association, vol. 69, no. 4, 2020, p. 451. doi: 10.1080/24750158.2020.1831900
7. Dana Williams and Marissa López, 'More than a Fever: Towards a Theory of the Ethnic Archive', Modern Language Association, vol. 127, no. 2, 2012, p. 358. doi: 10.1632/pmla.2012.127.2.357
8. Andrew Flinn, 'Archival Activism: Independent and Community-Led Archives, Radical Public History and the Heritage Professions', InterActions: UCLA Journal of Education and Information Studies, vol. 7, no. 2, 2011, p. 12. doi: 10.5070/D472000699
9. Sarah Welland and Amanda Cossham, 'Defining the Undefinable: An Analysis of Definitions of Community Archives', Global Knowledge, Memory and Communication, vol. 68, no. 8/9, 2019, p. 624. doi: 10.1108/GKMC-04-2019-0049; Amanda Lourie, Nina Kojovic, Katrina Hodgson and Mahnaz Alimardanian, 'Native Title Archives: Traditional Owner Community Owned and Controlled Repositories', Journal of Colonialism and Colonial History, vol. 20, no. 2, 2019, p. 2. doi: 10.1353/cch.2019.0020
10. Rebecka Sheffield, 'Community Archives', in Heather MacNeil and Terry Eastwood (eds.), Currents of Archival Thinking, Libraries Unlimited, Exeter, UK, 2017, p. 353.
11. Kirsten Thorpe, 'Aboriginal Community Archives', p. 900; Timothy Powell, 'The Role of Indigenous Communities in Building Digital Archives', in Ivy Schweitzer and Gordon Henry (eds.), Afterlives of Indigenous Archives, Dartmouth College Press, Hanover, New Hampshire, NH, 2019, p. 24.
12. Tahu Kukutai and John Taylor (eds.), 'Data Sovereignty for Indigenous Peoples: Current Practices and Future Needs', in Indigenous Data Sovereignty: Towards an Agenda, Australian National University Press, Canberra, 2016, p. 2. Raymond Lovett, Vanessa Lee, Tahu Kukutai, Donna Cormack, Stephanie Carroll Rainie and Jennifer Walker, 'Good Data Practices for Indigenous Data Sovereignty and Governance', in A. Daly, S.K. Devitt and M. Mann (eds.), Good Data, Institute of Network Cultures, Amsterdam, 2019, p. 26; Tahu Kukutai and Maggie Walter, 'Indigenous Data Sovereignty: Implications for Data Journalism', in Liliana Bounegru and Jonathan Gray (eds.), The Data Journalism Handbook: Towards a Critical Data Practice, Amsterdam University Press, Amsterdam, 2021, p. 65.
13. Maggie Walter, Raymond Lovett, Gawaian Bodkin-Andrews and Vanessa Lee, Indigenous Data Sovereignty Briefing Paper 1, Miaim Nayri Wingara Data Sovereignty Group and the Australian Indigenous Governance Institute, 2018, available at Indigenous+Data+Sovereignty+Summit+June+2018+Briefing+Paper.pdf (squarespace.com), accessed 21 April 2021.
14. Ibid.
15. Stephanie Carroll, Desi Rodriguez-Lonebear and Andrew Martinez, 'Indigenous Data Governance: Strategies from United States Native Nations', Data Science Journal, vol. 18, no. 31, 2019, p. 5. doi: 10.5334/dsj-2019-031
16. Ibid, p. 6.
17. Ibid.
18. Ibid.
19. Maggie Walter, Raymond Lovett, Gawaian Bodkin-Andrews and Vanessa Lee, Indigenous Data Sovereignty Briefing Paper 1, Miaim Nayri Wingara Data Sovereignty Group and the Australian Indigenous Governance Institute, 2018, available at Indigenous+Data+Sovereignty+Summit+June+2018+Briefing+Paper.pdf (squarespace.com), accessed 21 April 2021.
20. Stephanie Carroll, Ibrahim Garba, Oscar Figueroa-Rodríguez, Jarita Holbrook, Raymond Lovett, Simeon Materechera, Mark Parsons, Kay Raseroka, Desi Rodriguez-Lonebear, Robyn Rowe, Rodrigo Sara, Jennifer Walker, Jane Anderson and Maui Hudson, 'The CARE Principles for Indigenous Data Governance', Data Science Journal, vol. 19, no. 1, 2020, p. 6. doi: 10.5334/dsj-2020-043
21. Ibid, p. 1.

22. Stephanie Carroll, Desi Rodriguez-Lonebear and Andrew Martinez, 'Indigenous Data Governance: Strategies from United States Native Nations', Data Science Journal, vol. 18, no. 31, 2019, p. 10. doi: 10.5334/dsj-2019-031; Tahu Kukutai and Maggie Walter, 'Indigenous Data Sovereignty: Implications for Data Journalism', in Liliana Bounegru and Jonathan Gray (eds.), The data Journalism Handbook: Towards a Critical Data Practice, Amsterdam University Press, Amsterdam, 2021, p. 69.
23. Global Indigenous Data Alliance, Who We Are, Global Indigenous Data Alliance, 2022, available at gida-global.org, accessed 30 August. 2022.
24. Ibid.
25. Maiam Nayri Wingara Aboriginal and Torres Strait Islander Data Sovereignty Collective, About Us, Maiam Nayri Wingara Aboriginal and Torres Strait Islander Data Sovereignty Collective, 2017, available at https://www.maiamnayriwingara.org/about-us, accessed 20 April 2021.
26. National Centre for Indigenous Genomics, Annual Report 2021, About NCIG, Australian National University, 2021, available at NCIG-Annual-Report-2021.pdf (anu.edu.au), accessed 30 August 2022, p. 1.
27. Ibid.
28. Maiam Nayri Wingara Aboriginal and Torres Strait Islander Data Sovereignty Collective, About Us; see also Shannon Faulkhead, Livia Iacovino, Sue McKemmish and Kristen Thorpe, 'Australian Indigenous Knowledge and the Archives: Embracing Multiple Ways of Knowing and Leeping', Archives and Manuscripts, vol. 38, no. 1, 2010, p. 39.
29. Robert K. Yin, Case Study Research: Design and Methods, 6th ed., Sage, Thousand Oaks, CA, 2018.
30. Shawn Wilson, Research Is Ceremony: Indigenous Research Methods, Fernwood Publishing, Winnipeg, Manitoba, 2008, pp. 70–71.
31. Donna L. M. Kurtz, 'Indigenous Methodologies: Traversing Indigenous and Western Worldviews in Research', AlterNative: An International Journal of Indigenous Peoples, vol. 9, no. 3, 2013, p. 220. doi: 10.1177/117718011300900303
32. Michael Anthony Hart, 'Indigenous Worldviews, Knowledge, and Research: The Development of an Indigenous Research Paradigm', Journal of Indigenous Voices in Social Work, vol. 1, no. 1, 2010, p. 4.
33. Ibid.
34. Karen Martin and Booran Mirraboopa, 'Ways of Knowing, Being and Doing: A Theoretical Framework and Methods for Indigenous and Indigenist Research', Journal of Australian Studies, vol. 27, no. 76, 2003, p. 205. doi: 10.1080/14443050309387838
35. Maggie Walter (ed.), 'Glossary', in Social Research Methods, 4th ed., Oxford University Press, Melbourne, 2019, p. 18.
36. Robert Yin, Case Study Research: Design and Methods, 6th ed., Sage, Thousand Oaks, CA, 2018.
37. Jennifer Greene, Mixed Methods in Social Enquiry, Josey-Bass, San Francico, CA, 2007, p. 13.
38. Michelle Bishop, '"Don't Tell Me What to Do" Encountering Colonialism in the Academy and Pushing Back with Indigenous Autoethnography', International Journal of Qualitative Studies in Education, vol. 34, no. 5, 2020, p. 367. doi: 10.1080/09518398.2020.1761475
39. Roxanne Bainbridge, 'Autoethnography in Indigenous Research Contexts: The Value of Inner Knowing', Journal of Australian Indigenous Issues, vol. 10, no. 2, 2007, p. 55.
40. Andrew Junor, Significance Assessment of the Archive of the Koori Resource and Information Centre, Shepparton, Sue Hodges Productions, Port Melbourne, 2009, p. 8.
41. Ibid.
42. Ibid.
43. Ibid.
44. Richard Broome, Fighting Hard: The Victorian Aborigines Advancement League, Aboriginal Studies Press, Canberra, 2015.
45. Junor, Significance Assessment of the Archive of the Koori Resource and Information Centre, p. 20; Kaiela Institute, About Us, Kaiela Institute, 2022, available at https://www.kaielainstitute.org.au/about-us.html, accessed 30 August 2022, para 3–4.
46. Junor, Significance Assessment of the Archive of the Koori Resource and Information Centre, 2009, p. 20.
47. Tui Crumpen, Memorandum of Understanding between the Goulburn Valley Regional Library Corporation and the Koori Resource and Information Centre, Koori Resource and Information Centre, Shepparton, 2006, p. 2.
48. Junor, Significance Assessment of the Archive of the Koori Resource and Information Centre.
49. Ibid, p. 3.
50. Ibid, pp. 33–6.
51. Kaiela Institute, About Us, Kaiela Institute, 2020, available at https://www.kaielainstitute.org.au/about-us.html, accessed 6 December 2020, para 3–4.

52. The Fitzroy Stars (located in Thornbury) are the only other Indigenous owned and operated football and netball club in Victoria.
53. Junor, Significance Assessment of the Archive of the Koori Resource and Information Centre, p. 4.
54. Michelle Caswell, Alda Allina Migoni, Noah Geraci and Marika Cifor, '"To Be Able to Imagine Otherwise": Community Archives and the Importance of Representation', Archives and Records, vol. 38, no. 1, 2017, p. 1–22. doi: 10.1080/23257962.2016.1260445
55. Ibid, pp. 5 & 18.
56. Lyndon Ormond-Parker and Robyn Sloggett, 'Local Archives and Community Collecting in the Digital Age', Archival Science, vol. 12, 2011, p. 192. doi: 10.1007/s10502-011-9154-1
57. Jimmy Zavala, Alda Allina Migoni, Michelle Caswell, Noah Geraci and Marika Cifor, '"A Process Where We're All at the Table": Community Archives Challenging Dominant Modes of Archival Practice', Archives and Manuscripts, vol. 45, no. 3, 2017, p. 209. doi: 10.1080/01576895.2017.1377088
58. Definition of ID-GOV given to interviewees: 'Indigenous Data Governance is the management and organisation of information and data about us and our rights to collect, store, access and use that information and data according to our interests and cultural values'.
59. These documents formed part of the data sourced from the KRIC Archives. Koori Resource and Information Centre, Archiving Standards: Policy and Procedures Manual, KRIC Archives, Kaiela Institute, Shepparton, 2007a; Koori Resource and Information Centre, Rules for the KRIC Indexing System, KRIC Archives, Kaiela Institute, Shepparton, 2007d.
60. Koori Resource and Information Centre, Archiving Standards: Policy and Procedures Manual, Koori Resource and Information Centre, KRIC Archives, Kaiela Institute, Shepparton, 2007a.
61. Ibid.
62. Martin Nakata, 'The Cultural Interface', The Australian Journal of Indigenous Education, vol. 36, 2007, pp. 7–14. doi: 10.1017/S1326011100004646; see also Martin Nakata, 'Indigenous Knowledge and the Cultural interface', in Anne Hickling-Hudson, Julie Mathews and Annette Woods, Disrupting Preconceptions: Postcolonialism and Education, Post Pressed, Flaxton, 2003, pp. 19–38; see also Martin Nakata, 'Indigenous Knowledge and the Cultural Interface: Underlying Issues at the Intersection of Knowledge and Information Systems', IFLA Journal, vol. 28, 2002, pp. 281–289. doi: 10.1177/034003520202800513
63. Samantha Muller, '"Two Ways": Bringing Indigenous and Non-Indigenous Knowledges Together', in Jessica Weir (ed.), Country, Native Title and Ecology, ANU E Press, Canberra, 2012, p. 73.
64. Cyril Hedoin, 'Weber and Veblen on the Rationalization Process', Journal of Economic Issues, vol. 43, no. 1, 2009, pp. 170, 174 & 177. doi: 10.2753/JEI0021-3624430108
65. Kirsten Thorpe, The Dangers of Libraries and Archives for Indigenous Australian Workers: Investigating the Question of Indigenous Cultural Safety, International Federation of Library Associations and Institutions, vol. 47, no. 3. 2021, p. 1.
66. Jeanette Bastian, 'Radical Recordkeeping: How Community Archives Are Changing How We Think About Records', in Susan Mizruchi (ed.), Libraries and Archives in the Digital Age, Palgrave Macmillan, New York, NY, 2020, p. 81.
67. Martin Nakata and Marcia Langton (eds.), 'Introduction', in Australian Indigenous Knowledge and Libraries, UTSePress, Sydney, 2005, pp. 3–7; Martin Nakata, 'Introduction to the Special Issue: Engaging with Indigenous Knowledge, Culture and Communities', Australian Academic and Research Libraries, vol. 45, no. 2, 2014, p. 78. doi: 10.1080/00048623.2014.917785; Sarah Baker and Zelmarie Cantillon, 'Safeguarding Australia's Community Heritage Sector: A Consideration of the Institutional Wellbeing of Volunteer-Managed Galleries, Libraries, Archives, Museums and Historical Societies', Australian Historical Studies, vol. 5, no. 1, 2020, p. 72. doi: 10.1080/1031461X.2019.1659836
68. Sue McKemmish and Michael Piggott, 'Toward the Archival Multiverse: Challenging the Bianry Opposition of the Personal and Corporate Archive in Modern Archival Theory and Practice', Archivaria, vol. 76, 2013, p. 113.
69. Ibid, p. 133.
70. Jodi Bruhn, 'Identifying Useful Approaches to the Governance of Indigenous Data', PhD thesis, The University of Notre Dame, Sydney, 2013, p. 4.
71. Maggie Walter, Raymond Lovett, Gawaian Bodkin-Andrews and Vanessa Lee, Indigenous Data Sovereignty Briefing Paper 1, Miaim Nayri Wingara Data Sovereignty Group and the Australian Indigenous Governance Institute, 2018, available at Indigenous+Data+Sovereignty+Summit+June+2018+Briefing+Paper.pdf (squarespace.com), accessed 21 April 2021.
72. Andrew Flinn, 'Archival Activism: Independent and Community-Led Archives, Radical Public History and the Heritage Professions', InterActions: UCLA Journal of Education and Information Studies, vol. 7, no. 2, 2011, pp. 13–14. doi: 10.5070/D472000699

ARTICLE

On 'Holding the Process': Paying Attention to the Relations Side of Donor Relations

Jennifer Douglas*

School of Information, University of British Columbia, Vancouver, Canada

Abstract

This article reports on a series of interviews with archivists and recordkeepers conducted as part of a larger project exploring relationships between grief and recordkeeping. Though the interviews were not explicitly focused on donor relations, it emerged that the relationship between archivists and donors was a particularly emotionally charged one: interview participants described deep and complex relationships with donors, whom they often knew over a long period and through difficult or complicated times. Interview participants also reported feeling unprepared for this emotional work. This article responds to a perceived lack of attention paid to donor relations in archival theory and education by acknowledging the significance of donor stories, feelings and relationships. Aligned with the ever-growing emphasis in archival theory and praxis on person-centered approaches, the article suggests where such approaches are needed in relation to archival education and training, the collection and preservation of donor stories, relationship-building, and recognition of different kinds of archival labor.

Keywords: *Archival profession; Donor relations; Donors; Emotions; Grief*

Introduction

This article draws on a series of interviews with archivists and other records professionals conducted as part of a larger project exploring relationships between grief and recordkeeping. The Conceptualizing Recordkeeping as Griefwork: Implications for Archival Theory and Practice (2017–2023) project sought to understand the ways that grief might underpin or be otherwise involved in the creation, keeping and preservation of archives, primarily through interviews with archival creators and with archivists and records professionals. The interviews discussed in this article focused not only on how grief was part of or impacted archivists' work but also addressed other emotions involved in archival work; how prepared archivists felt for the emotional dimensions of their work; and what resources existed to support archivists working with emotional materials and people.

A prominent theme throughout these interviews related to archivists' interactions with donors. Although donor relations were not an explicit focus of the research project, it emerged that the relationship between archivists and donors was a particularly emotionally charged

*Correspondence: jen.douglas@ubc.ca

one: interview participants described deep and complex relationships with donors, whom they often knew over a long period and through difficult times, such as at the end of a career or the death of a loved one, and with whom they engaged in complicated and sensitive conversations and negotiations. Interview participants who emphasized the emotional nature of donor relations also described feeling unprepared for these relationships, pointing to education programs that emphasize the mechanics of acquisition by focusing, for example, on the transfer of materials into the legal custody and administrative purview of an archival institution without consideration for the relationships and feelings that are associated with or result from the transfer.

This article responds to the scant attention paid to donor relations in archival theory and education by acknowledging the significance of donor stories, feelings and relationships as themes that emerged from research on grief and other emotions in and as part of archival work. Aligned with the ever-growing emphasis in archival theory and praxis on person-centered approaches, the article suggests where such approaches are needed in relation to archival education and training, the collection and preservation of donor stories, relationship-building, and recognition of different kinds of archival labor. As Itza Carbajal argues in an article on 'the politics of being an archival donor', 'current archival paradigms tend to focus more on the archival materials than the people behind them'.[1] This article argues for a shift from this type of transactional and extractive emphasis toward attention to people, feelings, relationships and care.

Talking about archivists and donors

Recent articles on archival donors by Rob Fisher and Carbajal, and the only monograph on archival donors, by Aaron D. Purcell, discuss the ways that 'donors as a stakeholder group remain overlooked in archival donation programs, as well as in archival scholarship'[2]; they are, Fisher asserts, 'largely absent from our professional discourse'.[3] In a review of Purcell's book, Geof Huth, suggests that this absence might speak to how archivists 'have determined that donor relations is a simple and obvious practice that requires little skill'.[4] As a 'guidebook for successful programs', Purcell's book focuses on developing that skill (or set of skills). He provides a framework for professional archivists working with donors through a series of steps including initial contact, negotiations, examination of potential donations (e.g. site visits), appraisal and the drafting of donor agreements, and transfer of materials. Surveying the literature on donors in their 2009 article, Geoff Wexler and Linda Long note that it largely 'focuses on the technicalities of donor relations, such as legal precautions, accurate recordkeeping, and appraisal of material on-site'.[5] While Purcell's book includes a chapter on 'donor types' and attempts a categorization of donors (including 'the unassuming', 'the rich and famous', 'the sick and elderly', and 'the difficult, demanding, and non-donors'),[6] its presentation as a 'guidebook' means that it also tends to focus on what Wexler and Long might call 'technicalities' – or the 'how to' – of donor relations.

Other writing on donors discusses the development of relationships with donors, often in the sense of how archivists might work to establish or improve relationships with different individuals and communities in order to diversify their collections,[7] secure additional funding and resources,[8] or collaborate on projects to improve description and increase access to materials.[9] Wexler and Long's article is notable for delving deeply into Long's experience of working with ill and dying donors; the article considers the close relationships that can develop between an archivist and a donor and impact the acquisition process. Carbajal, who argues that much of the archival literature on donors tends to 'position donors as a means for acquiring more things', makes a case for more reciprocal and collaborative relationships between donors and archivists that empower donors to participate in broader decision-making about their records, while Fisher stresses the agency donors have to influence archival practices. While early research sometimes framed donors as the cause of archival 'problems',[10] Carbajal and Fisher remind us that donors are people, with complex motivations for donating archives and agency to assert their needs and desires. Although the archival literature is moving in the direction of engaging more deeply with the nature of donor relations, as the authors cited here agree, scholarly and professional writing on donor relations is limited in extent and scope and more research is needed to fill this gap. Although the Conceptualizing Recordkeeping as Grief Work project did not set out to study donor relations specifically, this article seeks to address this gap at least in part by sharing the perspectives of a number of archivists working with donors.

Methodology
The interviews discussed in this article were conducted between May and September 2019 with 29 participants who responded to an open call for archivists and other records professionals to talk about grief and archival work. The interviews, which were approved by the University of British Columbia's behavioural research ethics board, followed a semi-structured interview protocol, where participants were provided in advance with a series of questions related to how grief was involved in participants' work with donors and creators, with records, with records subjects and with researchers; about other emotions involved in these types of work; about how prepared participants felt for the emotional dimensions of archival work; and about any relevant resources they found helpful, as well as about resources they wished existed.[11] During the interviews, additional related questions were asked to clarify or add detail and participants were encouraged to ask questions and to direct the conversation as needed to share their own experiences and stories.

Three project research assistants and I transcribed the interviews, and transcripts were returned to participants for approval, at which time participants were also invited to make any additions or deletions to the transcripts as they felt appropriate or necessary; two participants did not return transcripts at this point, meaning 27 participant transcripts were included in the data analysis. Thematic coding of these transcripts was carried out with an expanded research team that included two additional research assistants using a codebook we developed through an iterative process and that included both structured and emergent codes.[12]

In this article, I pay particular attention to codes related to archivists' relationships and work with donors. Donors – and the relationships archivists had with donors – figured prominently in the interviews; 24 of the 27 participants discussed working with donors, and across the transcripts, the code 'relationships with donor and creators' was used 141 times and the code 'donor emotions and experiences' 156 times. In the sections that follow, I pay special attention to the research team's analysis of these two data codes to explore themes related to donor stories, feelings and relationships. Although several interview participants consented to be named in published findings, others did not and in the remainder of this article I use an alphanumeric coding system to refer to participants; in these codes, the letters indicate the type of archival position held by the interviewee (Table 1).

It should be noticed that archivists and recordkeepers self-selected to participate in the project, and that they participated because the topic of grief in and related to recordkeeping resonated in some way for them. The research discussed here was exploratory in nature, focused on particular experiences, and engaged with participants interested in those experiences. As I suggest throughout this article, more research will be needed with a broader focus on donor relations to fully understand the motivations and feelings of donors and the relationships that archivists form with them; this article opens one window onto these aspects of donor relations through its particular focus on grief.

Table 1. Participant codes

UA = University or college archives or equivalent
ASE = Archival scholar/educator
PA = Provincial or territorial archives or equivalent
MA = Municipal archives or equivalent
CA = Community archives
SA = School (K-12) archives

Talking with archivists about donors

When asked about where and how they encountered grief and other emotions as part of their work, many participants called special attention to working with donors during acquisition of archival materials and to maintaining donor relations. They explained how these processes can be laden with emotion, including but certainly not limited to feelings of grief and sorrow, and discussed how generally unprepared they felt to work in emotionally charged contexts. Although the interviews did not specifically set out to explore the relationships between donors, their materials, and the archivists who work with them, as such a frequent topic of conversation, these aspects of archival work merit special attention. In this section, I discuss four thematic groupings identified during the analysis of interview transcripts and related to: (1) the kinds of triggering life events that lead to donation; (2) feelings associated with different aspects of the donor-archivist relationship; (3) the nature of those relationships; and (4) the significance of donor stories.

Triggers

'Records don't change hands without some kind of trigger. And often those triggers are not necessarily happy ones.' [PA3]

Catherine Hobbs notes that when private donors work with archival institutions they are 'personally transferring [their] records as part of [their] very own life' and reminds archivists that archival donation is 'usually a highly personal and emotional transaction'.[13] Several of the archivists I spoke with reinforced the intimate and emotional aspects of appraisal, acquisition and donor relations, often describing how the process tended to be *triggered* by some kind of emotionally difficult life event, as for example the end of a career, the closing of an organization or association, illness and/or death of the donor or someone cared for by the donor.

Wexler and Long's important reflection on working with dying donors is one of few articles that directly engage with ageing, illness and death in archival work. Wexler and Long argue that archivists should be better prepared to work with ageing and dying donors because archival work is 'intimately bound up with these life events'. Archivists work with 'people at the end of their lives' and with 'those who are left behind – widows and widowers, lovers and partners, siblings, relatives and friends, not to mention colleagues and loyal employees, executors, and lawyers'.[14] The nature and effects of this kind of 'mediator deathwork'[15] were discussed in the interviews I conducted. For example, four participants described attending to donors on their deathbeds, explaining that it seemed important to the donors to talk to 'their archivist' before they died, sometimes to make sure their records would be understood and cared for, and sometimes because they wanted to 'sit and just talk' [UA1] with someone with whom they had, over time, developed an important, long-term relationship. Engaging directly with the concept of death work, some participants identified the archivist's role in 'facilitating a good end' [CA1], a role that is discussed in more detail below, but that for the archivist involves both reassuring the donor that their archives will be cared for and attending to the ending of the relationship.[16]

In addition to discussing the experience of attending at a donor's deathbed, participants described the impact of witnessing a donor's physical and mental decline in old age or due to illness. One participant who worked in a municipal archives [MA1] described their relationship with a community donor:

> I've watched him deteriorate, and I've found that very difficult. Because he was...he was such a vibrant member of the community and he's such a lovely man. And you know, I've sat at his house and his cat has sat in my lap, and I've developed a...a relationship with him. And then, they were just forced to leave their house and move into a retirement community, so he donated some more records [and] just watching him not be able to explain the records to me the way he did five years ago. I find that quite difficult.

Another archivist working at a provincial archives [PA1] described working with donors with terminal illnesses who were aware of having little time left to ensure the safe keeping of their records and legacy. This archivist referred to a phone call they 'will always remember':

> He phoned one day. I don't even really remember what about. He was just... he did a lot of work. He was a very interesting person. And I remember he said to me, 'You can't imagine what it's like, to not have enough time left to do everything you want to do'. And he died shortly after, and we got the last set of records.

They added, 'You meet a lot of people at difficult times in their life, for sure'. [PA1]

Triggers for records donation also include the end of a donor's career. Several participants discussed this type of trigger, with one archivist who worked in a university setting [UA1] explaining that some donors approach the end of their career 'very positively', while others 'find it very, very difficult to go through their papers and give them away. Because they know they're closing a door on something'.

A similar type of 'door closing' trigger is the end of an organization or association. Some participants described organizations that meant a great deal to those who worked for them but that could no longer be sustained, due to financial difficulty, a lack of volunteers and/or societal change; one archivist working for a large city archives [MA2], for example, described working with 'organizations that are wrapping up because they no longer have a place, like IODEs[17] or things like that, where nobody joins them anymore', or because of a 'loss of physical spaces, buildings [and] communities'. As with people 'wrapping up' their careers, those responsible for the records of associations and organizations may have different attitudes toward the ending; while some may be pragmatic and eager to have the records off their hands, others may feel the loss more acutely. PA1 described working with the donors of the records of older women's organizations: 'these older ladies come in, and they bring the records, and they are *sad* [emphasized] that this isn't going to continue, and that...you know, it's something that they had found so vibrant and important, is – had fizzled, or died, really'.

Records enter archival care as the result of these various triggers that signal the end – or deterioration of – a life, a career, an organization or a community. Archivists 'often work with donors when they're most vulnerable' [ASE1]; UA1 suggested that the time that archivists work with donors – at the end of something or the transition into something new – is also in some ways 'their best time'. Donors may be 'at a time where they're really looking back and they're – they want to share'. This kind of sharing, UA1 felt, was a 'privilege' and one that came with many feelings, both for the donors and the archivists.

Feelings

'It's very rarely a happy occasion that prompts someone to donate records to an archives.' [PA1]
Records donation is, or at least can be, an emotional process; in the interviews, donor relations and acquisition were emphasized as feeling-inflected processes. Participants described a range of feelings felt both by donors and creators and by archivists.[18] Unsurprisingly, since grief was a focus of the research project, participants discussed feelings of grief experienced by donors, who might be mourning the end of a career, of a loved one's life, or of their own life. Several participants discussed how records donation can be understood as part of a grieving process – one of the ways that grieving donors integrate and 'grow accustomed to the absence of a person' [CA1].[19] Donors' grief may be particularly pronounced when they are grieving someone who died young and/or unexpectedly [CA2], but even when a records creator lived a long and fulfilling life, the acquisition process involves handing over materials that connect donors to their lost loved ones, the 'physical evidence of their past existence' [CA1].

Living creators negotiating the transfer of their records may feel a similar kind of grief: 'even when people are downsizing, they're going through, like, a period of having to let go of, of that grief…and it's difficult. You can see they're not quite sure how to let go of it, they don't know what to do with it' [UA2]. Living creators, UA2 added, may experience a certain level of concern and anxiety about what will happen to their records: 'they're very concerned about the material being lost. And that, as well, it's almost like they're losing a part of themselves'.

One archivist working in a university archives [UA6] described feelings they encountered in donors during the acquisition of a community organization's records, noting that grief and other feelings of loss over records are not only felt as a result of a loved one's death:

> It's almost like, a sense of loss of community, that I see…just the fact of them donating the records and seeing, as the years go by, this incremental loss of membership. And trying— and like, failed attempts to try and bring more people in and to continue this thing that's been going on for decades. And then it's like, the final moment of donating it to the archives. Like, we tried everything and we failed. […] And our community failed. That it's really hard to, kind of, deal with that feeling… every time I've come across it in a community's records. In talking with donors or even the accession records, I always come across this great sense of loss, almost failure, from donors, that they could not keep the organization going, or feeling as if their communities have abandoned them or left them behind.

One participant who worked in a university archives [UA2] spoke at some length about how archivists have tended to neglect donor feelings. Acknowledging that archivists are often working with people experiencing loss of some kind, this participant suggested:

> I don't think we've ever really thought about it [deeply]. It's more like, treated as an acquisition process. So, you know, someone comes in, they want to donate, [and we say,] 'Okay, here we go, here's your deed of gift'. But we never stop and sort of slow down and think about…you know, we're dealing with the estate, we're dealing with the executor, or we're dealing with someone's family member. And so I'm not sure if we're always as…as respectful as we could be in the sense that we're dealing with someone who has passed away.

'We tend to be a bit cold-hearted', they added, focusing on policies and procedures instead of on 'the significance of these items to the person who is donating them' and how they feel about giving the material away. This participant [UA2] spoke about the importance of validating donor feelings, and recounts an incident where they had been, as they later saw it, insensitive with a donor by suggesting some materials had no archival value: 'And that upset her. Like she was in tears over it. And as I reflect back on it, I'm realizing now I was very insensitive in saying that they had no value. They had value because it was how she reflected her self-worth'. This archivist recognized the ways that records triggered memories for donors of important times in their lives or represented aspects of their past selves that held deep significance. UA2 felt that archivists are 'missing out on the symbolism' of records, and worried that what we profess about the value of records as reflections of a creator's life is not reflected in our policies and procedures, and especially in how we interact with donors.

Other participants described similar interactions with donors where they had misunderstood or not realized the significance of either the materials or the interaction. MA1 talked about a donor who continued to bring materials into the archives over a period of time. 'She kept bringing things and just asking me to do on-the-spot appraisals at the counter' MA1 recounted, explaining how they had to tell the donor repeatedly that the material did not have permanent value for the archives. 'But what I realize, now', MA1 shared, 'is that she was dealing with the death of her mother, and this was the way she was dealing with it'. Although MA1 was unsure what the archivist's responsibility might be in a scenario like this, they recognized that the donor's feelings needed to be acknowledged and understood.

One archivist working in a small, local archives [MA3] emphasized this need to acknowledge donor's feelings, identifying this as a key role that archival institutions and archivists play:

> You're called upon fairly regularly to minister people, and often it is some form of grief. And it's not always the usual form of grief, like they've lost a person. Sometimes it's the loss of their youth, the loss of their former life, the loss of what they see as their heyday or their prime…you know, when elder people move from a large place that had all their stuff around them, and they move to a small place and they have to get rid of all that stuff, it's a death every single time, and for some it's hugely traumatic and if we develop a relationship with them and with their family where we continue to take things and sometimes we take things that everybody knows are just going to go right out the back door again, but still it's an acknowledgment.

Stories

'Story is sacred. If you're telling a personal story or your family's story, nobody has exactly that story that you are telling. It's yours and you're sharing it with me.' [UA5]

Referring to the type of listening archivists need to engage in, MA3 told a story about 'a woman who came in, literally clutching to her chest' a tattered and mass-manufactured print painting depicting a story from the Bible. MA3 continued:

> And it was faded, and worn, and had been hung on a wall for so long that all the corners had tears where the pushpins had held it to the wall. And her best friend had just passed away, and this [object] had hung over her couch for as many years as this woman could remember. And with tears streaming down her face, she asked us to put this in the museum to remember her friend.

This item was not a traditional record, but for the donor, it functioned as a record of her friend's life and of the depth of their friendship; without this story, however, the meaning and significance of the object as a record are utterly lost.

Donor stories – the stories donors tell about their records and their lives – were a prominent topic of conversation during the project interviews. 'They *really* tell me their stories', UA3 emphasized, while UA1 explained how important it can be for donors to make sure archivists have their stories straight. UA1 describes an instance where they were called to visit a donor just days before he died. 'All he did', UA1 explains, 'was sit there and talk to me, about all these stories…and I knew he was hoping that somewhere…like I would be able to take this and put it in his papers'.

The stories participants heard from donors recounted not only the kinds of details about a donor's life and recordkeeping habits that would end up in a biographical sketch or scope and content note but also stories about the emotional significance of records to the donor. One community archivist [CA2] described how the stories donors tell about their archives emphasize different details than archivists might start out looking for; house visits, she explained:

> usually start with sitting down and they will tell me their parents' life story, which can be very short or very long, and then we can walk around and they'll point at certificates on the wall, newspapers, photo albums, but they won't talk about the photo album as in 'this is the family photo album from 1950 to 1960', they'll say, 'oh, and this covers our family trips and we went on this family trip because my father worked really hard and we went to a conference…', and everything is tied to the emotion, it has very little to do with how many photos are in this album, what is there, what's their status, what's the preservation concerns, what am I going to do with it. It's very much an emotional walk through.

UA2 similarly emphasized how donors tell stories about what records mean to them; describing the acquisition of a professor's papers, she explained, 'we were going through her materials, her fonds, [and] it was interesting because everything had a special memory to her, and it was the way she viewed herself, through her records'.

These kinds of stories, about donors' lives, their records, and their significance can be told with urgency, with donors looking for someone to 'hold on to' them. A participant who worked as a school archivist [SA1] described this kind of storytelling: 'I've had somebody grab my arm on multiple occasions and be like "listen, here's where I used to live, this is what we used to do when I was a boy…."' Sometimes, as was the case in this example, the urgency is connected to a feeling there is no one besides the archivist who will listen; as SA1 added, 'they say, "I don't know who else to tell. My kids don't care"'. The archivist plays a particular kind of role as a listener, and is a receptacle for a specific kind of story; as another archivist who worked in a provincial archives [PA2] put it, 'a lot of donors…want to make sure the legacy of the person they knew and loved is, somehow – that the records themselves aren't just transferred, but that there's more to it'. The 'more to it' relates to the donor's or creator's story, to the way they will be remembered. UA3 talked about a donor and his partner's records. The records, UA3 explained, 'were a vital part of his partner's life and his relationship with his partner. And to preserve them was preserving the memory of that relationship and of him'. Donors, many participants emphasized, come to the archives with a real need to have stories heard, acknowledged, and validated. As UA3 suggested, donors look to archives to care for records in a way that honors the dead; listening to, acknowledging and passing on their stories is part of that honoring.

Interview participants identified two key challenges associated with donor stories; they called attention both to the potential difficulties of recording and preserving donor stories and to the emotional labor involved in listening. SA1, describing instances of alumni 'grabbing' her at events to share their stories, elaborated that this:

> puts me in a strange place because it's kind of an oral record, so do I go back to my office and desperately try to write down these things that are told to me, and over the course of the day [at an alumni event] I get five or ten of these. Do I ask them to come back to do a

proper oral history? It's this outpouring and this sense of responsibility, that they're giving me in essence their life story, and hold on to it, don't drop it!

UA2, who talked about how the records of a professor they worked with connected deeply to the professor's sense of self, also discussed how difficult it could be to preserve that connection: 'Nowhere was this captured in the records', UA2 explained, 'and so how do we, as archivists, say, okay, how do we capture this? Do we capture it? Where do we report it in the fonds? Or in the RAD[20] description or whatever it is that we're doing? And what is the significance of it?' Participants in this project described not having formal processes to record and preserve donor stories, and noticed how current descriptive standards do not make specific space for donor stories to be shared with researchers in finding aids. UA2 felt strongly that more needed to be done to 'capture' the emotional significance of records to their creators:

> We need to keep in sight that there is something fundamentally important, that, when they're looking at something, when they turn over the photograph and they say, 'This is what this means to me and this is why it's important', it needs to be captured. It's not just a paper, it's not just about grief or anything like that. It's about…some sort of, I don't know, like, continuity of humanity in a sense?

While they recognized how important it was to listen to and acknowledge donors' stories, participants also noticed the type of 'emotional labor', as CA2 put it, of engaging in this type of listening. Telling their stories can be difficult for donors. While some find the experience satisfying and rewarding, for others the experience is painful and full of grief. The archivist sometimes takes on what several participants described as a counselling or grief therapist role in these situations. An archivist working in a college within a university [UA5] described feeling like they had 'become kind of the sponge for all these stories', and although they felt that archivists had an almost 'sacred' responsibility to care for the stories and lives connected to archives, they recognized, too, the effects this weight of responsibility could have.[21] CA2 also discussed this weight, describing how they often became donors' 'go to person on all things'; donors were able to talk to them about their own lives or the lives of their loved ones and realized they were a good listener; CA2 explained, laughing, that 'it's because they can get me on the phone', but over time, listening can become a burden, and one that archivists may feel compelled to carry. 'I've not yet figured out how to say no, nor do I totally think I should, I don't want to disconnect. If I am their connection to the archives, to the [anonymized] community, I don't want to be responsible for severing that connection'.

The experiences shared by participants about listening to donor stories highlight the importance of these stories both to the donors and creators of archives as well as to the meaning of the records they leave behind; participants suggested that archives cannot, in many cases, be fully understood without the context of the stories donors tell about them. The interviews also revealed that participants lacked methods for recording and preserving stories, and that while they viewed their role as listeners – as witnesses to a life – as a privilege, they also recognized the emotional toll associated with this privilege.

Relationships

'…to listen to what it meant to him, to hear the stories of his lost partner – it just takes time; it is a relationship.' [UA3]

Discussions about the events that trigger archival donation, about the feelings associated with these triggers and with the acquisition process, and about the importance of listening to and acknowledging donor stories underscore the different ways that archivists and donors enter into relationships with each other as they experience difficult life events together and negotiate the transfer of sensitive materials. Recent scholarship in the archival field has highlighted the relational nature of archives and archival work. For example, in their work on radical empathy and archives, Michelle Caswell and Marika Cifor describe the different types of relationships archivists form and are accountable within including relationships with creators, donors, researchers, records subjects and other archivists.[22] Interview participants also stressed this relational nature of archival work, observing that acquisition processes often involve multiple conversations, and sometimes home and office visits, and that these conversations frequently continue past the acquisition stage as collections are processed, digitized and made available for research use. Archivists work closely with donors and as discussed here in the section on triggers, often through emotionally difficult and/or distressing times. Relationships develop between donors and archivists as they work together over long and sometimes challenging time periods.

'I have very, very strong relationships with my donors', UA1 stressed, describing how these 'relationships go over a long period of time'. 'You become the point person', UA1 said, 'you take care of your donors'. This archivist described how relationships developed over time, recounting house visits that included homemade muffins and porch conversations: '[this one donor] always baked us muffins and we'd sit there on her porch and we'd look at the daisies, and we'd talk about stuff, and then she'd – you know, and it really – like, at this point, she wasn't even talking about [her career and records] anymore. She was now talking about her grandkids and stuff'. PA3 also emphasized the importance of these types of non-records-related conversations: 'Sometimes our conversations are just about visiting. We're not "negotiating," we're creating a relationship'.

In some cases, UA1 has developed multi-generational relationships, getting to know and work with a donor's children and grandchildren as years passed. The potential depth of donor relationships is evidenced in the desire some donors have expressed to see UA1 in their final days. This wish made sense to UA1: 'we're the keeper of their history', they explained. 'We're the keeper of their legacy…we're really important to them'. UA1 talked about how the relationship between a donor and archivist involves a certain degree of one-sidedness that develops because the archivist has a particular kind of access to a donor's life: 'you actually know them more than they know you because [laughs] you're also in their papers, right? So you know…it's not – it's more of a one-sided relationship. I mean if I died, I don't know if they'd feel that badly, right? I know them better than they know me. And it's all about them. It's not about me when we – when I go visit them, or whatever. You know, it's about them'. Although UA1 understands their role as being in service to the donor, they also see some elements of reciprocity in the relationship, describing the 'life lessons' they have learned from donors: 'Some of the things I've learned about life have…have just been what donors have said to me about who they are. Whether it's work ethic, or, you know, just taking time to look at a flower…just the philosophies of life that I've been able to gain from them'.

Other participants also spoke about relationships with donors that included being part of preparations for their death and/or helping family members to grieve after the death of a loved one. One participant, who worked in a provincial archives with private donors, considered the role of the archivist in comforting creators and their loved ones at the end of life, explaining that it can be important for a 'family to witness the good conversations that are going on' and for both the creator and their loved ones to feel satisfied that records will be 'in a good place' and treated with care. [PA3]

One community archivist [CA1] described a particular kind of relationship between archivists and grieving donors, which they described as 'holding the process'. CA1 explained first how they worked in the same archives for 30 years. 'It's a long time', they said. 'You build up a lot of relationships, you lose a lot of friends, you go to a lot of funerals, you give – and this is really quite healing, if you do it properly – you get to stand up in memorial meetings and say some things about the person. And you're the only person who knows certain things. So that's a joy'. Noting both the sorrows and joys of long-term relationship, CA1 explained how they understood their role of 'holding the process':

> … there were the usual conventional things you do as an archivist – meeting and talking with the person, the widow, about the records and their meaning; taking only those she's ready to part with; remaining in touch and returning when asked, for further conversation and another set of material. Those choices are always hers, or indeed the family's, in another situation which comes to mind. You allow them at the end of the day to say 'Actually, we're going to hold onto these for the moment'. And then, when they're ready for the next step, you're there – when the next year or so comes along, and they're ready to release and share more, you are there. You are holding the process. When I say 'allow', I think what I mean is you allow yourself to let go of a personal or institutional need to acquire, to have a conclusion to a transaction, to have an institutional process come to an end. You allow yourself and the institution to serve their needs to grieve and to manage the personal transition from the living presence to the negotiated absence of the person and the physical evidence of their being.

Holding the process involves the archivist in a crucial aspect of grief work. Other interview participants spoke about relationships with donors that involved the archivist in a kind of witnessing and/or counselling role. UA5, who worked in the archives of a religious college and acknowledged the 'intergenerational harm' experienced in the community, stressed that 'these aren't just pieces of paper for these people. These are very important parts of their life, or their parents' lives that they're handing over. And so…maybe it comes back a bit to that idea of almost having a pastoral role or counselling – not that I would consider myself a counsellor but you kind of have to just be very attentive to what people – what people need in this job'. MA3, the archivist who accepted the Bible story painting, likewise stressed that archival work can involve an 'element of ministry'. While these two participants leaned on religious language and imagery, this was done to draw attention to the importance of acknowledging the significance of relationship, of paying attention to where people 'are at' when they come in to an archives, of 'just listening' [UA5].

The kinds of relationship building discussed by these participants takes time, and participants who discussed the importance of relationship building to donor relations acknowledged that it can be difficult to balance the time it takes to build relationships against the time required to complete their other work. One archivist working in a large university archives [UA7] talked about working with an aging donor, going through hundreds of boxes together, and feeling 'the tension' between 'the emotional stuff' and the 'problem-solving': 'I had all this other stuff to do', UA7 lamented. They elaborated:

> [The donor would] sometimes get lost in stories, you know, go on tangents….You know, she would start talking about her children, and everything, like, that was unrelated to what we're doing. And it was all very interesting and I was happy to listen to it all. But I…I had to get back to the work! So, it was just like, 'How are we going to actually get through all this?' And make [institution name redacted] happy, and the librarian happy, and keep *her* happy, and just manage all that?

UA3 addressed this tension on the archivist's time by questioning how institutions have identified the 'metrics of success'. This participant described the way that relationships develop over time as donors bring more materials in and tell her their stories. They talked about the importance of honoring the openness donors demonstrated in telling their stories and the trust they placed in the archivist to listen and care, even if the institution would not ultimately acquire the material. UA3 acknowledged that this was not always a perspective shared by the institution they worked for, or other similar institutions, where 'success' is measured by amount of materials acquired, processed, digitized and used. UA3 explained:

> So let's say I spent, you know, a significant amount of time with three people, none of which we took their papers. But if we had, that would have been time well spent. But because I didn't – because we didn't, that's not time well spent. It's not a measurable outcome. And I find it very hard not to spend that time when it is somebody who's just lost a partner, or who's just lost – had a loss. I'm just not going to rush them. I just can't do that. [I am going to be] listening to their stories.

UA3 talked about this kind of relationship work continuing past the point of acquisition, describing an experience with a donor who 'was wondering why we hadn't given the art work of his partner a conservation treatment…you know he wanted better care for the materials'. UA3 took his question to the conservator and then talked to him again: 'I spent a lot of time listening to him about what that meant to him. So, even if we couldn't do the conservation work – or what happened is it's going on a list to be done eventually – but that – to listen to what it meant to him, and to hear the stories of his lost partner…it just takes time – it is a relationship of a kind' and, UA3 argued, therefore needs to be handled in a sensitive way. If 'he sees that it's not well taken care of, it feels like the organization to which he donated them doesn't care about him or the relationship – like it would be hard not to see that they don't actually care about him or the relationships…And that's where, you know, I was trying….That's all I could sort of say is, I cared, and I will do the best I can to make sure that I can take it as far as I can'.

Implications for future scholarly and professional work

The experiences and stories explored across the four themes of triggers, feelings, stories and relationships have significant implications for the development of more person-centered and trauma-informed policies, procedures, education and training. Because this research project was not specifically focused on donor experiences and relationships, additional research is necessary to fully develop new theories and methodologies, but areas for consideration and future research can be sketched out, and here, I propose five key interventions.

Improving education and training

Several of the participants interviewed said they had some idea of how to work with dying or ill donors and their loved ones because of their own past experience of loss and bereavement. While personal experience of trauma, grief and/or other emotions can certainly help to prepare an archivist to work in difficult scenarios, this experience should not form the bulk of their preparation; it is unfair and unethical for education and training programs to fail to prepare students to work in emotionally difficult situations in the face of the growing evidence that these are a regular feature of archival work.[23] Students and trainees need to know that a great deal of archival work involves interpersonal interaction (counter to the idea that archivists all work alone in basements sequestered with their collections) and that these interactions can be emotionally complicated and/or difficult. Students and trainees need to be trained in cultural sensitivity and to practice cultural humility,[24] and prepared to work in trauma-informed ways.[25] Archival educators are beginning to develop curricula that include this type of preparation, for example, at the Archival Education and Research Institute (AERI) held in

Liverpool in July 2019, Anna Sexton described efforts at University College London to 'train, prepare and support' recordkeepers to work with traumatic records.[26] At AERI 2022, Henria Aton, Christa Sato and Wendy Duff discussed the co-teaching by archival studies and social work scholars of a 6-week workshop for archival studies students in the Master of Information program at University of Toronto.[27] Professional archivists and archival professional associations are also taking on some of the responsibility for preparing archivists to work in trauma-informed ways and with difficult records. Michaela Hart, Nicola Laurent and Kirsten Wright were among the first professional archivists to speak publicly about the effects on archivists of working with difficult materials and of the need for trauma-informed archival practices.[28] Their public speaking led to the creation of a professional workshop offered through the Australian Society of Archivists.

This type of education and training needs to be widespread, embedded into all archival studies curricula, and treated not as an additional feature but as a core competency; curricular change of this magnitude will require program- and institution-level commitment to change. Professional associations also need to continue the work of archival education and training programs so that professionals already in the field, whose education neglected these topics, are able to acquire knowledge and skills to work with difficult records and in difficult relationships, and so that professionals can continue to add to their knowledge and skills throughout their careers.

Developing ways of 'holding the process'

When Catherine Hobbs reminds archivists that people donating their records are leaving a part of themselves behind, she follows up with a reminder about the responsibility this creates. 'The archivist', she asserts, 'needs to respond appropriately to the emotion which surrounds importing to the archives the records of someone's life'.[29] Several interview participants echoed Hobbs' call to recognize the emotional attachment that donors have to the materials they are handing over. For example, Hobbs' concern is similar to CA1's emphasis on 'holding the process', which includes acknowledging attachment (both to records and to the people they are connected to) and facilitating a kind of 'letting go'.

Discussion of the archivist's role in this type of facilitation was a common thread across the interviews. As described here, 'holding the process' involves the archivist in a form of grief work; in certain scenarios, the archivist may be part of the process through which a donor 'negotiates the absence of the person and the physical evidence of their being'. Jennifer Douglas, Alexandra Alisauskas and Devon Mordell draw explicit links to recordkeeping as a kind of griefwork, showing how creating and interacting with records can be a means by which the bereaved continue relationships with their lost loved ones[30]; it makes sense that letting go of these materials requires a particular kind of acknowledgment or process, and this is an area that deserves more attention from archivists. More research is needed to better understand the experiences of donors and, subsequently, to develop caring and trauma-informed approaches to acquisition work and the training needed to implement them.

Preserving donor stories

The importance of the stories donors tell about their lives and records was emphasized in a majority of interviews, but it was unclear to what extent these stories were being preserved and – where appropriate – communicated. A core tenet of archival theory and methodology is the importance of preserving records' contexts and most of our work is aimed at doing so. Archival scholars have regularly argued that records on their own cannot tell whole stories; constituting a 'sliver of a sliver of a sliver'[31] of the whole, they act as 'touchstones'[32] for memory, requiring 'activation',[33] to move from 'evidence of me' to evidence of us.[34]

How and where to capture records' full contexts and stories is not clear, however. While donor-provided information is likely to be included in finding aids in biographical sketches and scope and content elements, the telling of detailed stories about records is not accommodated in current descriptive standards and these stories are not often shared with users in other forms.[35] Often, stories about records are heard by archivists during the accession stage and may be recorded in some form in an accession record or file; these types of materials are not always – or even often – available to researchers[36] and new accession standards do not include fields that encourage the capture of detailed records stories.[37] The significance that interviewees accorded to donor stories suggests that these require more deliberate care and that archivists should look at developing ways of preserving them where they have consent to do so.

Three community archivists [CA1, CA2 and CA3] interviewed for this project conduct oral histories with donors as part of their regular procedures; SA1 also mentioned conducting oral history interviews but acknowledged it was 'kind of a fly by thing' rather than being their usual practice.[38] The use of oral histories with creators and donors has been discussed in the archival literature; for example, Carmen Ruschiensky describes an oral history project at Concordia University, the aim of which was to 'integrat[e] donor interviews into archival practice' in recognition of the importance of donor stories to 'meaning-making' in archival collections.[39] Similarly, Robert G. Weaver and Zachary R. Hernández describe an evolving process to incorporate donor stories into arrangement and description workflows at the Southwest Collection at Texas Tech University's Southwest Collection/Special Collections Library (SWC/SCL). They explain how recording oral histories with SWC donors had been a regular practice for many years, but that these recordings were typically stored separately from the archives and seen as a way of creating a supplementary record; only more recently have archivists realized the potential associated with working directly with donors during arrangement and description, allowing their stories to inform arrangement and add richness to description, and ultimately, making the archival process more collaborative and 'democratic'.[40] The recording of donor stories is also integral to Jamie A. Lee's work with the Arizona Queer Archives and the Digital Storytelling & Oral History Lab, where, Lee asserts, storytelling is the archives' 'organising principle and practice'.[41] Archives, Lee argues, become 'accessible and knowable'[42] through the stories that are told about, in and through them.

The commitment to storytelling that archivists such as Ruschiensky, Weaver and Hernández, and Lee demonstrate could be more widely adopted in archival programs. The importance accorded by interviewees to donor stories suggests that more work is needed to develop means of hearing, recording, and preserving them. Donor stories also need to be shared (as appropriate) by linking them to or including them in finding aids and other descriptive tools.

Measuring 'success'
A recurring issue discussed by participants in these interviews related to the tension they felt between the need to complete their work 'efficiently' and the time it takes to nurture donor relationships and honor their stories and experiences. As UA3 put it, the institutions in which archival work is carried out need to rethink what is considered as 'measurable outcomes' and how productivity is defined. Marika Cifor and Jamie A. Lee explain the ways that archival work has become subject to neoliberalist 'market metrics', citing 'new emphases within the administration of public institutions on "cost efficiency" and "profitableness"'.[43] Raquel Flores-Clemons discusses the difficulties of 'keep[ing] a people-first approach' in institutional settings 'because you have to prioritize the needs of the organization that holds the collection',[44] while Michelle Caswell, Alda Allina Migoni, Noah Geraci and Marika Cifor show in their research on the affective impact of community archives that these types of metrics are affecting not only public institutions but also community-driven archival efforts, where

community archives are 'increasingly forced to articulate their value in tangible – and often quantitative – ways to funders in the prevalent neoliberal frameworks'.[45] Within these neoliberal frameworks, time that does not lead directly to tangible returns in terms of number of accessions or linear metres processed – in other words time that cannot be measured in direct outcome – may be considered wasted, inefficiently spent and/or non-fundable; however, participants in this research project identified time spent building relationships as an integral part of archival work.

In my own experience, when I advocate for richer description and person-centered archival practices, methods that require more time and attention than is currently granted to tasks, I am frequently met with resistance; this type of work is criticized as being impractical and difficult or even impossible to implement with the resources available in archival institutions. However, contributions to archival scholarship by practitioner-researchers point out that how archivists decide to allocate time and other resources is to some extent at least a matter of prioritization; for example, invoking Antonina Lewis' concept of 'archival fragility',[46] Danielle Robichaud argues that 'by focusing on comfortably familiar neoliberal deflections like time and resources, archival fragility side-steps meaningful, action-oriented change'.[47] In other words, maintaining the status quo is a choice archivists make that allows them to avoid change; this choice, Robichaud shows, is often at the expense of justice and equity-oriented work. In a similar vein, David James Hudson notes how discourses of 'practicality' condone and/or endorse hegemonic racial politics and white supremacy[48]; as he explains, 'our very expectations and assumptions about the practical character and value of our field subtly police the work we end up doing and supporting, the kind of questions we ask and conversations we have, [and…] our sense, more generally, of what useful and appropriate political interventions look like from the standpoint of our profession'.[49]

These discussions about neoliberalist creep and the white supremacy of the status quo highlight how, as both Flores-Clemons and Robichaud show, change needs to happen at structural levels; the kind of person-centered approaches advocated for in this article and in other recent archival scholarship depend not on gestures of kindness from individual archivists but rather on fundamental changes to institutional and systemic policies, standards and practices.[50]

Centering people and relationships
The conversations I had with archivists and recordkeepers about working with donors highlighted the importance of relationships and of person-centered approaches to archival work. Traditionally, archivists' attention has been focused primarily – and sometimes seemingly exclusively – on the record, meaning that archival scholarship and education has privileged research and teaching about acquisition and preservation over public service. Increasingly, however, attention is shifting toward the people who create, donate, use and/or are represented in records.[51] Projects such as Memory-Identity-Rights in Records-Access (MIRRA) in England, Find and Connect in Australia, and the Shingwauk Project in Canada have shown that centering the person documented in a record, rather than, or in addition to, the procedures or policies for managing the record, can help archivists and records professionals identify actions and processes that have the potential to inflict harm or retraumatize records users.[52] As Elizabeth Shepherd has expressed, there is a clear call from those impacted by recordkeeping decisions and processes and from recordkeepers themselves to move away from a 'culture of recordkeeping for compliance' to develop instead a 'culture of caring recordkeeping'.[53] The interviews discussed in this article show that a culture of caring recordkeeping includes care for the people from whom archives acquire materials.

Caring recordkeeping involves particular kinds of archival labor. The archivists and recordkeepers I spoke with emphasized the importance of listening, of taking time, of honoring people's experiences and stories, and of acknowledging that donors may be feeling complex and difficult emotions. Caring recordkeeping involves relationship building. Lee asserts that 'the archives is, becomes, and exists in relationships. Always in relation',[54] and drafts a manifesto for a 'radical hospitality' that would transform archival practice and inform 'new ways of being in the world together'.[55] Kimberly Christen and Jane Anderson advocate for a 'slow archives' approach that acknowledges the centrality of relationships to archival work. Drawing on their work to develop archival systems and interfaces that 'center Indigenous temporalities, relationships and geographies', they ask how 'embodied, intimate, kin-based, land-based affective practice[s] of listening, sensing, remembering, making and remaking' can be foregrounded in archival processes.[56] Slowing down, they argue, is not only about taking more time, and it is certainly not in opposition to getting the work done. It is, fundamentally, a practice of 'focusing differently, listening carefully, and acting ethically' to privilege relationality as an archival logic.[57] Caswell and Cifor also place relationships – and people – at the center of archival theories and practices, arguing for a 'feminist ethics of care' that recognizes how archivists are 'caregivers, bound to records creators, subjects, users and communities through a web of mutual affective responsibility'.[58]

The interviews show that there is a need to shift thinking and teaching about donor relations from a fundamentally transactional approach to one that is more person-centered and that focuses on the relational aspects involved. As Dainan M. Skeem points out, the importance of emphasizing the *relations* aspect of donor relations is especially vital as archivists increasingly work with donors over long periods of time and through various stages of their careers. Archivists need to know not only how to start a relationship but also how to continue one.[59] A shift to prioritizing relationships will necessarily encompass aspects of 'holding the process', working on different timelines and reconsidering expectations and outcomes.

Conclusion

This article has explored themes related to triggering life events, feelings, stories and relationships in the context of archivists' work with donors, and has suggested that more work is needed to understand and prepare new archivists for the complex relationships that can exist between them and donors. The conversations I had with participants highlighted how changes to existing archival education and training programs, to institutional policies and procedures, to particular workflows and to inter-personal relationships require solutions at different levels across archival institutions, education programs, and professional associations. As Dorothy Berry has argued about reparative description and access, the kinds of systemic and structural changes required to shift archival education, institutional policies and professional practices to a person-centered model involve much more than a 'workflow adjustment'.[60] Projects such as MIRRA and the Emotional Response to Archival Records project at the University of Toronto are looking at the roles of archival institutions in supporting records subjects and recordkeepers, respectively; additional research could look at the roles archival education programs and professional associations have to play in developing understanding of, and supporting recordkeepers involved in, the emotional dimensions of archival work.

The conversations I had with interview participants about donors occurred in a particular context – in a study on grief and other emotions in archival work – that will have impacted their nature and focus; a more broadly focused study on donor relations might reveal other characterizations of the work and experiences of the different parties involved. Furthermore, because the research described in this article was not explicitly focused on donor relations, more research is required to understand the nature of the different types of relationships that can develop between archivists and donors and the impact of relationships on the acquisition process. This article suggests several potential areas for future research – around education and training; holding the process; preserving donor stories; measuring success; and working in relationship – but these are by no means exhaustive.

Carbajal's assertion that 'current archival paradigms tend to focus more on the archival materials than the people behind them' is borne out by the archivists I interviewed. The conversations about donor relations that are explored here demonstrate a strong disconnect between the prominent focus on transaction and procedure in archival literature and education and the lived experiences of working archivists. This disconnect means that archivists are underprepared for the emotional dimensions of their work. 'That's something my archival education did not prepare me for', UA5 told me: 'The idea that I would be…that emotionally involved with people who were very emotional about their records'. This article argues for a shift from the types of transactional and extractive emphases evident in 'archival paradigms' toward attention to people, feelings, relationships and care. While more attention is beginning to be paid to the emotional dimensions of archival work, the eagerness of the archivists and recordkeepers who responded to the call to participate in this research project and other related projects, the high attendance at conference sessions on related topics, and the shift in archival theory toward affect, emotion and empathy all demonstrate that there is a great deal of more work to be done and that now is the time to do it.

Acknowledgements

This research conducted for this article was generously funded by the Social Sciences and Humanities Research Council (SSHRC) Canada through the Insight Development Grant (2017–23). I am deeply grateful to the 29 archivists and recordkeepers who shared their experiences with me during the summer and fall of 2019; thank you for your candour, your empathy and your trust. This research was helped along by an outstanding research team, including graduate research assistants Alexandra Alisauskas, Elizabeth Bassett, Noah Duranseaud, Ted Lee, Christina Mantey and Catherine Hall. Thank you to the two anonymous peer reviewers for your generous feedback, to the editorial team, and to the Australian Society of Archivists for your commitment to open access publishing.

Notes

1. Itza Carbajal, 'The Politics of Being an Archival Donor: Defining the Affective Relationship between Archival Donors and Archivists', Journal of Critical Library and Information Studies, vol. 3, no. 2, 2021, pp. 1–26, doi: 10.24242/jclis.v3i2.114.
2. Ibid.
3. Rob Fisher, 'Donors and Donor Agency: Implications for Private Archives Theory and Practice', Archivaria, vol. 1, no. 79, Spring 2015, p. 92.
4. Geof Huth, 'Review of Donors and Archives: A Guidebook for Successful Programs, by Aaron D. Purcell', The American Archivists, vol. 76, no. 1, 2016, p. 201.
5. Geoff Wexler and Linda L Long, 'Lifetimes and Legacies: Mortality, Immortality, and the Needs of Aging and Dying Donors', The American Archivist, vol. 72, no. 2, 2009, p. 479.
6. Aaron D Purcell, Donors and Archives: A Guidebook for Successful Programs, Rowman and Littlefield, Lanham, MD, 2015. See Chapter 7 on 'Donor Types'.
7. See for example, Jessica L Wagner and Debbi A Smith, 'Students as Donors to University Archives: A Study of Student Perceptions and Recommendations', The American Archivist, vol. 75, no. 2, 2012, pp. 538–66.
8. See for example, Elizabeth Konzak and Dwain P Teague, 'Reconnect with Your Alumni and Connect to Donors', Technical Services Quarterly, vol. 26, no. 3, 2009, pp. 217–25; Ben Primer, 'Resources for Archives: Developing Collections, Constituents, Colleages, and Capital', Journal of Archival Organization, vol. 7, no. 1–2, 2009, pp. 58–65.
9. See for example Andrea Payant, Becky Skeen, Anna-Maria Arnljots and Randy Williams, 'Beyond Crowdsourcing: Working with Donors, Student Fieldworkers, and Community Scholars to Improve Cultural Heritage Metadata', Journal of Digital Media Management, vol. 8, no. 3, 2020, pp. 242–253.
10. Barbara Kaiser, 'Problems with Donors of Contemporary Collections', The American Archivist, vol. 32, no. 2, 1969, pp. 103–7.

11. For a detailed overview of the project, see Jennifer Douglas, Alexandra Alisauskas, Elizabeth Bassett, Noah Duranseaud, Ted Lee and Christina Mantey, '"These Are Not Just Pieces of Paper": Acknowledging Grief and Other Emotions in Pursuit of Person-Centred Archives', Archives & Manuscripts, vol. 1, no. 50, 2022, pp. 5–29.
12. A more detailed discussion of the work of the research team can be found in [removed for anonymization].
13. Catherine Hobbs, 'The Character of Personal Archives: Reflections on the Value of Records of Individuals', Archivaria, vol. 2, no. 52, Fall 2001, pp. 132–3.
14. Wexler and Long, 'Lifetimes and Legacies', p. 478.
15. 'Mediator deathwork' is a term used by death studies scholar Tony Walter, who explores types of professional work that involve a professional mediating between the dead and the public, often through some form of public rite. Examples he discusses include coroners, funeral directors, obituary writers, mediums and museum curators. Archivists could also be included in this list as they translate their knowledge of a deceased creator to create appraisal reports, finding aids, exhibits, etc. Tony Walter, 'Mediator Deathwork', Death Studies, vol. 29, no. 5, 2005, pp. 383–412.
16. In Wexler and Long, 'Lifetimes and Legacies', Long discusses her experience working with and caring for a donor at the end of the donor's life.
17. IODE stands for International Order of the Daughters of Empire.
18. Recent work across several research projects has explored archivists' 'emotional responses' to working with records and the people who create, donate, use and are documented in them. See Cheryl Regehr, Wendy Duff, Henria Aton and Christa Sato, '"Humans and Records Are Entangled": Empathic Engagement and Emotional Response in Archives', Archival Science, vol. 22, 2022, pp. 563–83; Jennifer Douglas, Alexandra Alisauskas, Elizabeth Bassett, Noah Duranseaud, Ted Lee and Christina Mantey, '"These Are Not Just Pieces of Paper": Acknowledging Grief and Other Emotions in Pursuit of Person-Centred Archives', Archives and Manuscripts, vol. 50, no. 1, 2022, pp. 5–29.
19. Because the interviews conducted for the Conceptualizing Recordkeeping as Grief Work project were specifically focused on recordkeepers' experiences of grief, and because participants self-selected based on their interest in this topic or on the degree to which it resonated with them, our conversations emphasized grief as an aspect of archival work, including in donor relations. New research on donors might address what Duff et al. are calling 'emotional responses' more broadly and uncover other experiences or emphasize different feelings.
20. RAD, *Rules for Archival Description*, is the Canadian description standard.
21. This participant's metaphor of the story 'sponge' and her characterization of archival listening as a 'sacred' duty calls to mind Jamie A Lee's self-description as 'the storytelling receptionist and concierge'. Lee, too, describes the effects of being 'touched, moved and changed' through every conversation and story and represents archives as 'a space of reception that turns itself into a sacred resting place. Jamie A Lee, 'Archives as Spaces of Radical Hospitality', Australian Feminist Studies, vol. 36, no. 108, 2021, p. 156.
22. Michelle Caswell and Marika Cifor, 'From Human Rights to Feminist Ethics: Radical Empathy in the Archives', Archivaria, vol. 81, Spring 2016, pp. 23–43.
23. Recent work on secondary trauma and archivists and on the emotional dimensions of archival work confirm that experience of working with difficult materials and in difficult situations is widespread. See Katie Sloan, Jennifer Vanderfluit and Jennifer Douglas, 'Not "Just My Problem to Handle": Emerging Themes on Archivists and Secondary Trauma', Journal of Contemporary Archival Studies, vol. 6, 2019, p. 20, available at https://elischolar.library.yale.edu/cgi/viewcontent.cgi?article=1090&context=jcas, accessed 2 February 2023; Duff et al., 'Humans and Records Are Entangled'; Douglas et al., 'These Are Not Just Pieces of Paper'.
24. Jessica Tai, 'Cultural Humility as a Framework for Anti-Oppressive Archival Description', Journal of Critical Library and Information Studies, vol. 3, no. 2, 2021, pp. 1–23, doi: 10.24242/jclis.v3i2.120; Kirsten Thorpe, 'The Dangers of Libraries and Archives for Indigenous Australian Workers: Investigating the Question of Indigenous Cultural Safety', IFLA Journal, vol. 47, no. 3, 2021, pp. 341–50; Kristen Thorpe, 'Transformative Praxis – Building Spaces for Indigenous Self-Determination in Libraries and Archives', In the Library with the Lead Pipe, January 23, 2019, available at https://www.inthelibrarywiththeleadpipe.org/2019/transformative-praxis/, accessed 10 February 2023.
25. Kirsten Wright and Nicola Laurent, 'Safety, Collaboration, and Empowerment: Trauma-Informed Archival Practice', Archivaria, vol. 91, Spring 2021, pp. 38–73.
26. The program for this institute is no longer available online.
27. Henria Aton, Christa Sato and Wendy Duff, 'Trauma-Informed Approaches to Information: Reflections on Co-Teaching an Innovative 6-Week Master's Level Workshop', Paper Presented at Archival Education

and Research Institute, July 14, 2022, online, http://aeri.website/events/category/virtual-aeri-2022/2022-07/, accessed 15 May 2023.
28. Nicola Laurent and Michaela Hart, 'Emotional Labor and Archival Practice: Reflection', Journal of the Society of North Carolina Archivists, vol. 15, 2018, pp. 13–22.
29. Hobbs, 'The Character of Archives', p. 133.
30. Jennifer Douglas, Alexandra Alisauskas and Devon Mordell, '"Treat Them with the Reverence of Archivists": Records Work, Grief Work, and Relationship Work in the Archives', Archivaria, vol. 88, Fall 2019, pp. 84–120.
31. Verne Harris, 'The Archival Sliver: Power, Memory, and Archives in South Africa', Archival Science, vol. 2, no. 1, 2002, p. 65.
32. Laura Millar, 'Touchstones: Considering the Relationship between Memory and Archives', Archivaria, vol. 61, Fall 2006, pp. 105–26.
33. Eric Ketelaar, 'Tacit Narratives: The Meanings of Archives', Archival Science, vol. 1, no. 2, 2001, p. 138.
34. Sue McKemmish, 'Evidence of Me', Archives & Manuscripts, vol. 24, no. 1, 1996, pp. 28–45.
35. See Jennifer Douglas, 'Toward More Honest Description', The American Archivist, vol. 79, no. 1, Spring/Summer 2016, pp. 26–55.
36. Kristan Cook and Heather Dean discuss the types of information gathered and documented in accession files and consider how this information could be of use to researchers; they explain how the benefits of researcher access to this material are balanced against donors' privacy and suggest how filing practices in archival repositories can ensure that material that can be viewed by researchers without risk is made available. See Kristan Cook and Heather Dean, 'Our Records, Ourselves: Documenting Archives and Archivists', in Kathleen Garay and Chritl Verduyn (eds.), Archival Narratives for Canada: Re-Telling Stories in a Changing Landscape, Fernwood, Halifax and Winnipeg, 2011, pp. 56–73.
37. See, for example, the Canadian Archival Accession Information Standard, available at https://archivescanada.ca/wp-content/uploads/2022/12/CAAIS_2019May15_EN.pdf, accessed 22 November 2022.
38. It must be noticed that I did not ask specific questions about these practices, so it is possible that more participants were conducting oral history interviews as part of ad hoc or regular procedures.
39. Carmen Ruschiensky, 'Meaning-Making and Memory-Making in the Archives: Oral History Interviews with Archives Donors', Archivaria, vol. 84, Fall 2017, p. 106.
40. Robert G Weaver and Zachary R Hernándea, 'Oral History, Donor Engagement, and the Cocreation of Knowledge in an Academic Archives', Archivaria, vol. 1, no. 93, Spring 2022, p. 75.
41. Lee, 'Radical Hospitality', p. 157.
42. Lee, 'Radical Hospitality', p. 158.
43. Marika Cifor and Jamie A Lee, 'Towards an Archival Critique: Opening Possibilities for Addressing Neoliberalism in the Archival Field', Journal of Critical Library and Information Studies, vol. 1, no. 1, 2017, pp. 1–22, doi: 10.24242/jclis.v1i1.10.
44. In Ashley D Farmer, Steven D Booth, Tracy Drake, Raquel Flores-Clemons, Erin Glasco, Skyla S Hearn and Stacie Williams, 'Toward an Archival Reckoning', The American Historical Review, vol. 127, no. 2, June 2022, p. 807.
45. Michelle Caswell, Alda Allina Migoni, Noah Geraci and Marika Cifor, '"To Be Able to Imagine Otherwise": Community Archives and the Importance of Representation', Archives and Records, vol. 38, no. 1, 2017, p. 10.
46. Antonina Lewis, 'Omelettes in the Stack: Archival Fragility and the Aforeafter', Archivaria, vol. 2, no. 86, Fall 2018, pp. 44–67.
47. Danielle Robichaud, 'Integrating Equity and Reconciliation Work into Archival Descriptive Practice at the University of Waterloo', Archivaria, vol. 1, no. 91, Spring 2021, p. 101.
48. Drawing on critical race theory, Hudson explains how 'whiteness' dominative power resides, in crucial part, in its occupation of a space of unmarked normativity'. It 'persists through an ability to assert its historical peculiarity and precarity as timeless, universal, and neutral'. It is the 'mythical norm' (quoting Audre Lorde) that librarians and archivists protect and continue when they appeal to practical reasons why they cannot act to create change in policies and procedures. David James Hudson, 'The Whiteness of Practicality', in Gina Schlesselman-Tarango (ed.), Topographies of Whiteness: Mapping Whiteness in Library and Information Studies, Library Juice Press, 2017, pp. 203–234.
49. Hudson, 'Whiteness of Practicality', p. 205.
50. Michelle Caswell and Marika Cifor, 'Revisiting a Feminist Ethics of Care in Archives', Journal of Critical Library and Information Studies, vol. 3, no. 2, 2021, pp. 1–6, doi: 10.24242/jclis.v3i2.162.

51. See the special issue of *Archivaria, Toward Person-Centred Archival Theory and Praxis*. The editor's introduction suggests a definition of *person-centred* and traces some of its lineage through archival literature and professional practice. Jennifer Douglas, Mya Ballin and Jessica Lapp, 'Introduction', *Archivaria*, vol. 94, Fall 2022, pp. 5–21.
52. For more information about the MIRRA project see, for example: Elizabeth Shepherd, Victoria Hoyle, Elizabeth Lomas, Andrew Flinn and Anna Sexton, 'Towards a Human-Centred Participatory Approach to Child Social Care Recordkeeping', Archival Science, vol. 20, no. 4, 2020, pp. 307–25; Victoria Hoyle, Elizabeth Shepherd, Andrew Flinn and Elizabeth Lomas, 'Child Social-Care Recording and the Information Rights of Care-Experienced People: A Recordkeeping Perspective', The British Journal of Social Work, vol. 49, no. 7, 2019, pp. 1856–74.

    For information about Find & Connect and the impact of understanding Care Leaver experiences on recordkeeping practices see: Joanne Evans, Frank Golding, Cate O'Neill and Rachel Tropea '"All I Want to Know Is Who I Am": Archival Justice for Care Leavers', in David A Wallace, Wendy M Duff, Renée Saucier and Andrew Flinn (eds.), Archives, Recordkeeping and Social Justice, Routledge, London, 2020, pp. 105–26.

    For information on the Shingwauk Project and the Shingwauk Residential Schools Centre see: Krista McCracken, 'Community Archival Practice: Indigenous Grassroots Collaboration at the Shingwauk Residential Schools Centre', The American Archivist, vol. 78, no. 1, 2015, pp. 181–91; Krista McCracken and Skylee-Storm Hogan, 'Residential School Community Archives: Spaces of Trauma and Community Healing', Journal of Critical Library and Information Studies, vol. 3, no. 2, 2021, pp. 1–17, doi: 10.24242/jclis.v3i2.115.
53. Elizabeth Shepherd, 'Care Leavers: "Trying to Access Childhood Records Is Distressing and Dehumanizing"', The Conversation, October 3, 2019, available at https://theconversation.com/care-leavers-trying-to-access-childhood-records-is-distressing-and-dehumanising-124381, accessed 10 February 2023.
54. Lee, 'Radical Hospitality', p. 157.
55. Lee, 'Radical Hospitality', p. 161.
56. Kimberly Christen and Jane Anderson, 'Toward Slow Archives', Archival Science, vol. 19, 2019, p. 90.
57. Christen and Anderson, 'Slow Archives', p. 90.
58. Caswell and Cifor, 'From Human Rights to Feminist Ethics', p. 24.
59. Dainan M Skeem, 'Donor Relations in the Twenty-First Century', Journal of Western Archives, vol. 9, no. 1, 2018, article 9.
60. Dorothy Berry, 'The House that Archives Built', up/root, June 22, 2021, available at https://www.uproot.space/features/the-house-archives-built, accessed 7 March 2023.

ARTICLE

Green Ribbon and Blue Ribbon Stories: Applying a Bidjara Way of Knowing to Understanding Records

Leann Wilson[1] and Rose Barrowcliffe[2,*]

[1]Regional Economic Solutions, Brisbane, Australia; [2]Department of Indigenous Studies Macquarie University, Sydney, Australia

Abstract

Archival turn scholars have argued that to understand a record one needs to consider its broader provenance. Theoretical and conceptual frameworks such as the record continuum model, parallel provenance and societal provenance have aided in debunking the myth of linear, objective and neutral records. While these theories and concepts support the inclusion of Indigenous worldviews in recordkeeping praxis, Indigenous worldviews have been noticeably absent in the formulation of these and other archival theorisations. This article introduces the green ribbon and blue ribbon stories, an Indigenous, specifically Bidjara, conceptual framework for appraising and interpreting archival records. This conceptual framework has been derived from Bidjara ways of being and knowing. This article consists of three parts: the first introduces the conceptual framework and explains its background. The second discusses the intellectual and cultural authority of the framework and protocols for its use, and the final part of the article demonstrates how the green ribbon and blue ribbon stories' conceptual framework applies to archives.

Keywords: *Bidjara; Green ribbon and blue ribbon stories; Provenance; Traditional Knowledge attribution; appraisal; Traditional Knowledge ownership*

Preface (Rose Barrowcliffe)

In 2021, I attended a Building on the Strengths of our Stories' cultural strengths workshop held online for Queensland State Archives (QSA) staff. The training was co-developed by Bidjara/Kara-Kara and South Sea Islander woman Leann Wilson (co-author of this paper) and her colleague, Charlene Berndt (who is Kamilaroi with family links to Kokoberra). The training explores some of the key issues of Queensland's history relating to Aboriginal and Torres Strait Islanders. To do this, Leann, Charlene and their co-facilitators introduce the green ribbon and blue ribbon stories, a conceptual framework formulated by Leann and drawn from her family's teachings about Bidjara Country. The green ribbon and blue ribbon stories (explained in detail in Part 1 of this article) provide a framework for exploring issues through both Indigenous and non-Indigenous worldviews. As I listened to Leann and Charlene explain

*Correspondence: rose.barrowcliffe@mq.edu.au

the green ribbon and blue ribbon stories, I grew more and more excited. I could see how it could be used as a conceptual framework to be applied to understanding archival records.

After the training, I searched for the green ribbon and blue ribbon stories in academic publications. I wanted to use them in my research and as an academic, I wanted to use academic citations to ensure that Leann was properly attributed as the intellectual property (IP) holder. I found no mention of the green ribbon and blue ribbon stories in academic publications, so I contacted Leann and asked if she had published them anywhere. When Leann said that she had not published it anywhere I asked if I could support her in doing so. Happily, Leann was as keen to see the green ribbon and blue ribbon stories published as I was, and this article is the result of our collaborative efforts conducted through yarning and writing.

Publishing the green ribbon and blue ribbon stories' conceptual framework triggered a host of concerns about how to preserve and protect Leann's intellectual and cultural rights over the knowledge. As an Aboriginal academic, I am keenly aware of the problematic history of appropriation of Indigenous knowledge by academics. Academic, legal and cultural notions of knowledge ownership differ, and this article mediates these three paradigms. As excited as I am that Leann has agreed to publish the green ribbon and blue ribbon stories, I also feel a weight of responsibility in ensuring that Leann does not lose ownership and control of the green ribbon and blue ribbon stories through the publication process. Academic research has a long history of extraction and benefit hoarding when it comes to publication of Indigenous knowledges and non-Indigenous IP laws, such as copyright law, protect those that publish knowledge, even if it is not their own knowledge that they publish.

Extractive research can occur even when the researcher is Indigenous. I did not want this article to be another example of that so I carefully considered how to ensure that Leann remains the sole cultural authority and IP owner of the green ribbon and blue ribbon stories, even though this article is co-authored. As a Butchulla person, I am aware that the green ribbon and blue ribbon stories are connected to Bidjara culture and that I have no authority to share it without Leann's permission. Rather than wanting to share the conceptual framework on Leann's behalf, I want to support her in sharing it. Despite being a co-author on this paper, I claim no ownership of the green ribbon and blue ribbon stories conceptual framework or any of the Bidjara stories shared in this article. The rights for the green ribbon and blue ribbon stories conceptual framework and Bidjara stories remain entirely with Leann.

To bring this article to fruition, we have followed cultural and academic protocols. As the academic, I was tasked with the writing. I drafted this article after yarning sessions with Leann. The reader only sees the text-based authorship of this process, but this article was authored orally in those yarning sessions. Perhaps in another time, or with another researcher, this would have been a single-authored paper based on those yarns, but Leann's cultural authority underpins this article and that is recognised in the article's structure and citation format. We have drawn on the latest citation practices that recognise Indigenous knowledge and cultural authority. We make clear who has authored each section of the article. Not only does this make the speaking position clear, but it is also a way to protect Leann's IP and cultural authority in relation to the green ribbon and blue ribbon stories. We encourage all users to follow the citation guide below if you want to use the green ribbon and blue ribbon stories' conceptual framework in your research (which we sincerely hope you do).

Leann Wilson
Co-founder, Regional Economic Solutions
Leann Wilson is a descendant of the Thompson family of the Bidjara/Kara-Kara and South Sea Islander peoples. She grew up with her Thompson family in and around Barcaldine on

Bidjara Country. Leann is the co-founder of Regional Economic Solutions that support Indigenous communities, governments and businesses nationally to broker understanding and co-design agreements. Leann also co-designed the award-winning Building on the strength of our stories training that teaches Queensland history through the lens of Aboriginal and Torres Strait Islander lived experience affected by the successive Queensland legislation that impacted Aboriginal and Torres Strait Islander peoples. Leann's work spans community, government, not-for-profit, education and private enterprise.

https://www.linkedin.com/in/leann-wilson-a79b323b/

Rose Barrowcliffe (corresponding author)
Postdoctoral Research Fellow, Centre for Global Indigenous Futures, Macquarie University
Rose Barrowcliffe is a Butchulla postdoctoral research fellow at Department of Indigenous Studies and the Centre for Global Indigenous Futures. Rose's research examines the representation of Indigenous peoples in archives at both an organisational level and record level. Rose is the inaugural First Nations Archives Advisor to the Queensland State Archives and is an active member of the Indigenous Archives Collective.

https://orcid.org/0000-0003-1958-5507

Twitter: @BarrowcliffeR

https://www.linkedin.com/in/rose-barrowcliffe/

The TK (Traditional Knowledge) Notice is a visible notification that there are accompanying cultural rights and responsibilities that need further attention for any future sharing and use of this material. The TK Notice may indicate that TK Labels are in development and their implementation is being negotiated.

Local Contexts Project ID: bd9cd164-c282-4c36-96a2-1f485d67a25b

Citation: Leann Wilson (Bidjara) & Rose Barrowcliffe (Butchulla). 'Green ribbon and blue ribbon stories: Applying a Bidjara way of knowing to understanding records', Archives and Manuscripts, vol 50, no 2, 2022. doi: 10.37683/asa.v50.10921

Both authors are recognised in the citation for this article, as per academic convention, but to maintain the correct cultural authority of the green ribbon and blue ribbon stories conceptual framework, Part 1 of this journal article should be cited as:

Leann Wilson (Bidjara) in Leann Wilson (Bidjara) & Rose Barrowcliffe (Butchulla). (2022). Green ribbon and blue ribbon stories: Applying a Bidjara way of knowing to understanding records. *Archives and Manuscripts,* vol 50, no 2, 2022. doi: 10.37683/asa.v50.10921

INTRODUCTION

Archival records have long been defined, appraised, described and interpreted through a colonial worldview. Post-modern archival theorists introduced notions of non-linear histories and multiple provenances to archival theory, but Indigenous-developed frameworks are still largely absent in mainstream archival praxis. This journal article introduces the green ribbon and blue ribbon stories' conceptual framework, which is underpinned by Bidjara[1] teachings. The framework has synergies with the records continuum model and societal and parallel provenance but is unique due to its Bidjara ontological and epistemological underpinnings.

This journal article consists of three parts: the first part introduces the green ribbon and blue ribbon stories' conceptual framework. The second part of the article goes into detail about the intellectual property (IP) rights and protocols for the use of this conceptual framework. The final part of the article discusses how the green ribbon and blue ribbon stories can be applied as a framework to appraise, describe and interpret records. Each of the three parts of this article was deliberated on separately and then brought together holistically in this article because the production and attribution of knowledge are inherently connected to the understanding of that knowledge.

Protecting cultural authority was a key focus throughout the writing and publication process, and in this article, we share the considerations and subsequent solutions we adopted for protecting the IP and cultural authority of the conceptual framework. To protect that cultural authority of the green ribbon and blue ribbon stories, we apply the latest practice in the academic citation for recognising Indigenous knowledges in academic writing. Part 2 of this article uses the green ribbon and blue ribbon stories to demonstrate the differences between legal authority, specifically copyright and IP ownership and cultural authority. While copyright and IP can be used to protect cultural authority in the short term, additional measures need to be taken to protect cultural authority in perpetuity.

The application of the green ribbon and blue ribbon stories provides archival practitioners, theorists and users with an Indigenous, specifically Bidjara, framework for appraising, describing and interpreting records. Part 3 discusses the similarities between the green ribbon and blue ribbon stories' conceptual framework and existing archival theories such as the records continuum model, parallel provenance and societal provenance. This article argues that while all records have multiple provenances, two specific provenances must always be considered for records in colonised nations like Australia: that of the Indigenous peoples (the green ribbon) and that of the coloniser (the blue ribbon).

By introducing a new conceptual framework and demonstrating how to apply it, we offer contributions to knowledge for both collecting institutions and academic publishing. The intersection of these two fields is the production and management of knowledge. This article demonstrates one possible pathway for producing and managing knowledge from an Indigenous worldview that is congruent to practices in collecting institutions and academia. Further, that any production of Indigenous Knowledge can and should occur with the cultural authority remaining intact, whether that be in an archival or academic setting.

Part 1: The green ribbon and blue ribbon stories of the Bidjara cave paintings
(Leann Wilson – Bidjara/Kara-Kara and South Sea Islander)

The history of Australia can be considered through two different time frames and ways of knowing: Indigenous and non-Indigenous. In this article, we introduce a conceptual framework that represents these two ontologies using two ribbons: one green and one blue. The green ribbon represents Indigenous ontologies that are based on Country, lore, deep time and the stories that Aboriginal and Torres Strait Islanders have known and passed down for tens of thousands of years. The blue ribbon represents the non-Indigenous ontologies, post-invasion history and the events that have occurred since the arrival of the British.

It helps to see this representation in a physical sense, not just as a metaphorical one. When I and my Kamilaroi and Kokoberra colleague, Charlene Berndt, deliver our Building on the Strengths of our Stories training, we bring actual green and blue ribbon into the training rooms for trainees to hold as they consider the history of Queensland. The green ribbon is 65 metres long, with each metre of ribbon signifying 1,000 years. The blue ribbon is just over 25 centimetres long. The blue ribbon is starkly short in comparison to the green ribbon, as is accurate when comparing the long Aboriginal and Torres Strait Islander history on this continent against that of the British. I explain how to apply the green ribbon and blue ribbon stories to understanding history by sharing the following story that has been passed down through my family.

On Bidjara country, in central-western Queensland, there are a series of caves that have been a woman's area for Bidjara women for tens of thousands of years. The caves, known as the Palace, contain paintings that hold Bidjara stories and record Bidjara history. Custodianship of this area has been passed down through Bidjara women for as long as this site has been significant to our people. The Bidjara women give lessons to the Bidjara men at the caves, but the Bidjara men have no authority over the caves. The Bidjara women's teaching is that women are best positioned to speak of all things to do with women and these gatherings of women and young boys start early in a young boy's life, well prior to the boys learning from the men.

In 1909, a group of non-Indigenous males came to Bidjara Country to examine the caves. It is believed that in a bid to assess their provenance and significance the visiting men questioned the Bidjara men about the cave paintings. According to Bidjara lore, the Bidjara men do not have cultural authority to speak about the caves or the paintings, so they told the visiting men that they did not know anything about them. From this interaction, the non-Indigenous men concluded that the paintings were not created by or known to the Bidjara.[2] However, that is an untruth and the story of the Palace must take into consideration both the green ribbon and the blue ribbon stories for the cave. The green ribbon story and the blue ribbon story of this place represent two different worldviews.

Any discussion about the history of the Bidjara cave paintings and their current state of being has seen the assumption that there is no knowledge and thus decisions and writings have excluded without balance and agency of the Bidjara women. The green ribbon story passed down from my grandmother in fact tells a story of the intersectionality of women's and men's business. The sacredness of birthing and burials unpacks the story of rights and responsibilities. In this case, the rights of women and the responsibility of the men in honouring and supporting the agency of women and girls were what prevented the men from speaking about the caves.

The green ribbon story passed down by my father is an example of this intersectionality in action. My father never spoke of, or about, the Palace. However, he knew of it and he understood implicitly his responsibility to Mother Earth, his mother, my grandmother and me. It is from this Bidjara knowing he taught us about 4R's. *4R.* was also the family horse brand, so lessons were reinforced each time we branded or saddled and rode our horses. My father spoke of these 4's, as the stories that underpin our way of knowing, being and doing, taught early to strengthen and ground the learner. The 4Rs include Remember your story, Respect, Relationships and Responsibility (for Mother Earth, self and others).

Part 2: Intellectual property protection and protocols for use of the green ribbon and blue ribbon stories' conceptual framework (Rose Barrowcliffe-*Butchulla*)

Protecting the Indigenous cultural and intellectual property (ICIP) of the green ribbon and blue ribbon story has been one of our greatest concerns in relation to this publication. Leann has worked for decades sharing and teaching Indigenous and non-Indigenous people about the importance of seeing history through both Indigenous and non-Indigenous worldviews, and this publication is a continuation of that work. In publishing the green ribbon and blue ribbon stories' conceptual framework here, Leann is encouraging its use; however, any use should recognise cultural authority of Leann as the developer of the concept and Leann's family as her teachers.

The process for authoring the journal article has allowed us to explore the intersections and misalignments between Indigenous and academic knowledge production and authority. In this section, we discuss where IP laws, particularly, copyright and creative commons (CC) licensing, fall short of protecting Indigenous Knowledge and cultural authority. To protect the Indigenous Knowledge contained within this article, and the cultural authority over the article, we considered a meld of different knowledge attributions formats including academic citation, Traditional Knowledge Labels (TK Labels) and IP licensing through copyright and CCs. In this section of the article, we explain our choices for attribution, and what they mean for the use of the green ribbon and blue ribbon stories' conceptual framework.

Authorship and citation

There are many examples over the years of Aboriginal and Torres Strait Islander people losing control of their knowledge once it is shared to the broader public.[3] Academic production of knowledge has long seen academics securing IP ownership of Indigenous Knowledge through the publication process.[4] A slow paradigm shift in academia has seen a move away from extractive research in favour of research done by, for and about Indigenous peoples. This work is being done by the increasing number of Indigenous researchers in academia who are growing the cultural interface within the academy. Not only is Indigenous scholarship within the academy increasing, but Indigenous scholars are changing the way that research is being conducted. Indigenous research methodologies,[5] and Indigenous research methods[6] are being increasingly practiced in academia, resulting in relational accountability[7] underpinning a growing number of research designs. Part of that relational accountability is recognising that knowledge produced in Indigenous communities deserves the same respect and protection as that produced within the academy. It is the responsibility of the academic to ensure this happens.

Supporting Indigenous knowledge governance and sovereignty in research and publishing is multi-faceted and needs to be considered during the various stages of knowledge production, from research design and execution to publication and peer review, and then to citation. Bennett[8] (Gamilaraay) argues that when writing about Aboriginal and Torres Straight Islanders, researchers should use literature written for and by Aboriginal and Torres Strait Islander researchers. In cases where it is still necessary to cite non-Indigenous sources, such as when critiquing legacy works, Nathan Sentance[9] (Wiradjuri) suggests retroactively adding to citations both the names of contributing Indigenous people, and their Nation, if known. The University of Technology Sydney[10] and James Cook University[11] have each updated their citation guides to include formats for attributing Indigenous knowledge, including retrospectively adding Indigenous co-contributors and their Nation name to academic citations. Lock et al.,[12] a group of Indigenous and non-Indigenous authors from 11 Indigenous nations (Ngiyampaa, Wiradjuri, Oglala Lakota, Gamilaraay, Ngāpuhi, Bkejwanong, Quandamooka, Bundjalung, Worimi, Nurrunga and Ngarrendjeri) and four colonial nations (Australia, New Zealand, USA and Canada) developed the Indigenous Cultural Identity of Research Authors Standard (ICIRAS), a guide for embedding indigenous identity in author credentials that also give several suggestions for structural change to the publication process.[13] The Indigenous Archives Collective (IAC) authored CAVAL Indigenous referencing guide for Indigenous knowledges (due to be published in May 2023) gives scholars a framework for first deciding which sources are appropriate and second how to appropriately attribute Indigenous Knowledge authority. All of these guides recommend clearly identifying Indigenous people by name and Nation, Country or language group name, if self-identified by the author, when using their knowledge in research publications. In this journal article, we use the author's name and their Nation/Country/Language group name, if known, in the initial in-text appearance and then again in the reference list.

It is important to name Indigenous Knowledge holders in academic publications' citations despite academic citation being an inadequate form of IP protection (discussed further in the next section). Without explicitly stated cultural identities in publications, there is an implied uniformity of cultural standpoints underpinning all research.[14] Including cultural identification of authors can assist both peer reviewers and readings in their appraisals of the rigour and cultural appropriateness of the research.[15] The ramifications of copyright go beyond academic publishing, in our discussions, we have been most concerned with the following reasons for asserting copyright:

- without being named in the citation, or identified in the body of the work, the Indigenous knowledge runs the risk of becoming an orphan work that cannot be connecting back to the community at a later date (libraries, museums and archives already hold many works like this in their collections);
- any knowledge, Traditional or otherwise, comes under the legal control of the named authors when it is published; therefore non-Indigenous researchers become the copyright holders and legal rights holders of any Indigenous Knowledge they publish under their own name;
- while copyright expires, it still provides legal protection for the knowledge published in the works for the life of the author plus 70 years;
- copyright holders are often the designated authority that decides the terms of donations to collecting institutions, including compensation, description and access[16];
- and while there are currently no adequate legal protections for Indigenous Knowledge, ICIP and systems like TK Labels are rapidly evolving and give hope that a solution will be available before the expiry or any copyright licensing commencing today.

Academic authorship has historically been distilled down to those that have physically written the publication and/or those that have been assigned roles within the research team.[17] This practice disadvantages Indigenous Knowledge holders who share their knowledge with researchers without being considered part of the research team or being involved in the writing process.[18] By academic conventions, this article may otherwise have been single authored by Rose Barrowcliffe based on interviews with Leann Wilson, but that would not have provided adequate recognition to the cultural authority of Leann. While this article has been drafted by Rose, the core knowledge shared in this article, the green ribbon and blue ribbon stories' conceptual framework, is the sole intellectual and cultural property of Leann. As mentioned in the preface, this article was first authored orally, and it is the cultural authority of the knowledge, not the mediums through which it is being published, that has determined the authorship of this article.

In addition to who is included in the citation, author order is also important in academic publishing. First authors' names are given greater prominence and may be more closely associated with the publication than second or later authors. In academia, first-authored publications are also weighted more favourably in considerations for promotions. The general rule for author order is that the person who contributes the most should be the first author, but author order can also be arranged alphabetically or in order of academic seniority. In the case of this article, Leann Wilson is placed as the first author in the citation format for this article. This author order recognises Leann as the person that formulated the framework, the significance of which supersedes that act of writing the article (the contribution of Rose Barrowcliffe). It also places more emphasis on the importance of cultural authority than the academic writing process. The decision to put Leann first was primarily made to ensure that the green ribbon and blue ribbon stories' conceptual framework will always be associated with Leann's name first and foremost, as is appropriate. In placing Leann as the first author, we go against academic citation norms and instead place Indigenous knowledge and cultural authority above academic authorship as the deciding factor for attribution in academic publication.

Copyright, CCs licensing and indigenous knowledge
Publishing the green ribbon and blue ribbon stories' conceptual framework has meant finding a balance between Indigenous forms of knowledge creation and ownership and non-Indigenous legal frameworks for IP protection. Copyright and CCs licensing, the most widely used forms of IP protection, both fall short in their ability to fully protect Indigenous Knowledge. Torres Strait Islander scholar Professor Martin Nakata[19] noted that when working within the cultural interface, Indigenous people often have to make choices according to the constraints and possibilities of the moment. In publishing this article, we are utilising these non-Indigenous IP legal frameworks to achieve an imperfect protection for the green ribbon and blue ribbon stories' conceptual framework. In this section, we explain the shortcomings of copyright legislation when using it to protect Indigenous Knowledge.

Copyright legislation is intended to protect 'original works'. The Copyright Act[20] and its subsequent regulations[21] define what types of original works copyright applies to, and the protection it can offer, but they do not specifically define the term 'original works'. The Commonwealth of Australia[22] and the Australian Copyright Council[23] define original works by the form of the works and the role of the creator. The works must be 'fixed in material form', whether that be electronic or hard copy, and the creator must be a human who has used their own 'intellectual effort' and 'requisite skill' to create a work that is not a copy of another's work.

The requirement of 'material form' reinforces the non-Indigenous underpinnings of the Copyright Act. Material forms include published literature, scripts, song lyrics, audio or visual recordings, emails or computer programs.[24] The problem is that for tens of thousands of years, Aboriginal and Torres Strait Islanders have recorded their knowledge in non-material forms such as songs and oral histories. Fixing Indigenous Knowledge in material form has often been undertaken by non-Indigenous people who do not give attribution to Traditional Knowledge holders. In many cases, this has resulted in the non-Indigenous author becoming the copyright owner of Indigenous Knowledge.[25] When Indigenous Knowledge enters copyright licensing through publication by people outside of their Traditional Owner communities, it results in the ongoing exclusion of Traditional Owners from the knowledge ownership cycle.[26] Where Indigenous Knowledge does exist in material form, such as paintings or artefacts, these material records seldom contain attributions to their individual creators. In the interpretations of original works by the Commonwealth of Australia and the Australian Copyright Council, these previous works fall outside of copyright protection and have been treated as public domain (discussed further in next section). The result is that Indigenous Knowledge, whether fixed in material or non-material form, is rarely recognised by copyright law as being the IP of its Indigenous creators.

Time frames of knowledge creation are the other incompatibility between copyright and Indigenous Knowledge ownership. The work becomes recognised as a complete, original work at the point of publication rather than being seen as a constantly evolving piece of knowledge. The end point of copyright licensing is also definitive, with the most common license term being for the life of the author plus 70 years. By comparison, Indigenous Knowledge ownership does not expire. What is even more alarming about this arbitrarily set expiration date is that it was not even decided by Australian law or people. The time periods for copyright licensing were handed to Australia from the government of the United States as part of Free Trade negotiations.[27]

In comparison to these restrictive definitions of knowledge creation and form, definitions of Indigenous Knowledge are much more expansive. Indigenous Knowledge is created through collective intellectual effort: it is a communal endeavour over long time periods rather than an individual one with a defined start and end date. Like other forms of original works, Indigenous Knowledge builds on existing knowledge that has been passed down over tens of thousands of years without proprietary ownership by individuals to any one piece of knowledge. Our methods of creating and safeguarding knowledge may be more akin to stewardship, but our attribution and benefit-sharing rights should be treated the same as those of non-Indigenous knowledge creators and owners. This tension between guardianship and ownership prompted this article into being. As guardian of the stories of the Bidjara caves and their paintings, Leann is responsible for protecting those stories. By publishing the green ribbon and blue ribbon stories, Leann's guardianship is now also recognised as ownership according to copyright law.

What is traditional knowledge and who owns it?

The debate about who owns Indigenous Knowledge and where it sits within the rights and moral obligations of IP law is intertwined with the notion of 'Traditional Knowledge'. As a legal and political term, 'Traditional Knowledge' was 'invented' along with the formulation of 'public domain' as part of the CCs movement.[28] James Boyle, author of Shamans, Software and Spleens: Law and the Construction of the Information Society,[29] which launched the CCs movement, argues that IP laws, including copyright laws, are so restrictive that they stymie innovation and creativity. The more nuanced CC licenses function in conjunction with the copyright license and are only valid as long as the copyright license is valid. Boyle uses examples of extraction of Indigenous Knowledge, which he refers to as 'Traditional Knowledge', to argue for more nuanced control on knowledge ownership. To support his argument, he gives the example of the extraction of medicinal knowledge from Indigenous peoples in the Amazon rainforest and Madagascar by large pharmaceutical companies. These companies use Indigenous knowledge to identify plants that have medicinal properties, they then commercialise the active ingredients without sharing any of the benefits with the Indigenous Knowledge holders. Boyle argues that the Indigenous Knowledge of the medicinal plants should not be able to be exclusively privatised by the pharmaceutical companies and that Indigenous people should share in the benefits of the commercialisation of their knowledge. Boyle connects protecting Indigenous Knowledge with environmental and cultural sustainability, arguing that financial rewards for sharing of their knowledge would support Indigenous peoples in continuing their medicinal, cultural and land use practices.[30] Boyle's argument is not that large pharmaceutical companies should not be allowed to extract, commercialise and profit from Indigenous Knowledge, but that if they are going to do so, the Indigenous Knowledge holders should benefit as well.

Sunder[31] takes exception to Boyle's formulation of Indigenous peoples as conservators of knowledge rather than IP holders. Sunder contests that Boyle's arguments for Traditional Knowledge to sit in the public domain frame Traditional Knowledge as 'raw material for innovation'[32] rather than innovation itself. Furthermore, Sunder argues that Indigenous people need to be seen not just as wardens of 'raw materials' (including Traditional Knowledge), but as being an active part of the knowledge production process. After all, IP is not just about knowledge products but also knowledge processes. Drawing on the World Intellectual Property Organization's 2006 report Intellectual Property and Traditional Knowledge,[33] Sunder argues that Indigenous Knowledge is not static, and therefore IP rights must also be applied to new developments in Indigenous knowledge. Sunder surmises that adaptation of Traditional knowledge to contemporary problems is not just pragmatic, it is a sign of a healthy and dynamic culture.

The term 'Traditional Knowledge' locks Indigenous knowledge production in the past. It indicates an invisible line drawn at the time of invasion to delineate knowledge created before invasion as 'Traditional' and everything since as something different. The truth is that knowledge is constantly evolving and the original knowledge today is the Traditional Knowledge of the future. Therefore, the original knowledge created today, and the original knowledge created in times past deserves the same amount of protection because the process of their development is the same.

The green ribbon and blue ribbon stories' conceptual framework is Sunder's argument in action; it is the Traditional Knowledge of Bidjara people adapted to the contemporary problem of trying to understand Australian history when there are multiple narratives. Though formulated over the past 30 years, the conceptual framework is underpinned with ancient Bidjara teachings, ways of knowing, doing and being. The green ribbon and blue ribbon stories' conceptual framework illustrates that though the Bidjara culture is ancient, it is not stagnant, and it is alive and evolving in current times. The green ribbon and blue ribbon stories' conceptual framework deserves the same rights and protections as long-held Traditional Knowledge.

Traditional knowledge (TK) Labels

Despite the limited time periods for IP protection under copyright law, the green ribbon and blue ribbon stories' conceptual framework will always belong to Leann and her family. An additional method of rights assertion is needed to support the perpetual ownership of the green ribbon and blue ribbon stories' conceptual framework as an original work of Indigenous (Bidjara) Knowledge that also recognises the long and continuing arc of Indigenous Knowledge creation. One possible solution to support perpetual rights attribution is the TK Labels created by Local Contexts.

Local Context Labels,[34] more commonly known as TK Labels, have been developed in collaboration with Indigenous communities and are an extra-legal layer of IP protection that provides attribution to the Indigenous Knowledge holders. TK Labels were born out of the realisation that archives 'radically fail' Indigenous communities.[35] Not only do Indigenous peoples not control their own cultural heritage in archives, but they often do not even have access to it. Archives and research are built on a tradition of 'extraction' and 'deliberate theft',[36] which results in data (knowledge held in records and materials) being collected and held with no provenance information.[37] TK Labels were created to address the lack of provenance in existing Indigenous Knowledge materials held in archives. They are a tool for Indigenous communities to reconnect their knowledge stored in archives back to their community.

The Local Context Labels apply the CARE (Collective benefit; Authority to control; Responsibility; Ethics)[38] to Indigenous data sovereignty[39] by building correct ownership attribution into the metadata of catalogues storing Indigenous Knowledge, but it is not always appropriate to use the labels. What is often referred to simply as TK Labels is in fact a system that combines three user profiles (Indigenous community, institution or researcher), two types of attribution (Traditional Knowledge (TK) or Bio-cultural knowledge (BC)) with two levels of attribution (labels or notices) to create a nuanced ICIP rights support mechanism.[40] TK Labels and BC *Labels* are used by Indigenous communities to clarify rights, interests, relationships and protocols of knowledge and bio-cultural information. TK Labels and BC Labels can only be created by Indigenous communities and are created and managed at a community/tribe/iwi level. TK and BC *Notices* are used by researchers and institutions to acknowledge Traditional Knowledge in their records and indicate their support for Indigenous rights and interests in relation to that knowledge. The TK Notices are unique in that they create a pathway for institutions and researchers to open the door to attribution without impinging on Indigenous knowledge owners 'authority to decide for themselves what the labels on the knowledge should be. They can also hold space for collaboration between institutions and Indigenous communities before they have established a relationship and can do so without pushing Indigenous communities to adhere to institution and researchers' timelines. The notices open the door to collaboration and relationship building and, when the partnership results in mutual trust, may eventually lead to TK/BC Notices being replaced with TK/BC Labels.[41]

Within the Local Contexts framework, this journal article is seen as a project between a researcher (Rose) and an individual Indigenous community member (Leann). Initially, we had hoped to use TK Labels to provide attribution to Leann and her family for the green ribbon and blue ribbon stories' conceptual framework. After gaining a fuller understanding of how the Local Contexts labels and notices operate, we have instead used a TK Notice (displayed at the beginning of this article before the abstract). In the case of this article, a TK Notice was more appropriate than a TK Label because Leann and I have worked at an inter-personal level rather than at a community level as required by Local Contexts. The TK Notice for this journal article indicates that there is Indigenous knowledge in the article that will continue to carry moral obligations long after the copyright and CC licensing expire. This is the first article to use TK Notices in an academic journal article (J. Anderson, personal communication, Feb 9, 2023) and demonstrates its application in academic publishing. Specifically, the use of the TK Notice in this article demonstrates the ability for researchers to make public disclosures about Indigenous knowledge that informs their research.

This article demonstrates one possible way that institutions and researchers can begin the process of connecting research data and archival records back to their Indigenous owners and cultural authorities. Non-Indigenous IP legislation remains an imperfect method of securing Indigenous Knowledge ownership rights. These rights relate not just to commercialisation of Indigenous Knowledge but also to the cultural protocols for the use of Indigenous Knowledge. Solutions like Local Context's TK Labels and Notices can fill gaps created by IP legislation. By using TK Notices, institutions and researchers can act according to their moral obligations to Indigenous knowledge owners without being held back by legislative limitations.

Part 3: Green ribbon and blue ribbon stories and archives (Rose Barrowcliffe)

In the Building on the Strength of our Stories workshops, Leann Wilson, Charlene and their colleagues use the green ribbon and blue ribbon stories' conceptual framework to understand Queensland history. To do this, they examine Queensland's post-invasion history through the successive legislation that directly impacted Aboriginal and Torres Strait Islanders and discuss the effect those pieces of legislation have had on Indigenous peoples' lives using specific examples from their own families. Issues like place names, Stolen Generations, stolen wages, Aboriginal and Torres Strait Islander health outcomes and more are discussed by considering the green ribbon stories (deep time, connection to Country, Indigenous Knowledge and lived experience) and blue ribbon stories (colonist legislation, non-Indigenous lived experience, colonial narratives) of these topics. This process of considering the multiple perspectives to a topic, and also the evolution of understanding of certain issues through the telling and retelling of a story has parallels with archival theories such as societal provenance,[42] parallel provenance[43] and the records continuum model.[44] These archival theories and concepts have been developed by and remain largely contained in the discussions of archival theorists. By comparison, the green ribbon and blue ribbon stories' conceptual framework has been developed from a lay user and Indigenous, specifically Bidjara, worldview. It is one that is easily translatable and understandable to archival theorists, practitioners and users alike and can be applied to any archival record or process.

Leann's family's story of the visitors to the Bidjara caves applies the green ribbon and blue ribbon stories to interpret both the original record and the pluralised record. The original record is the paintings that remain located in the caves on Bidjara Country. Derived from that is a new record, *The Queenslander* newspaper article published in October 1909. Using a records continuum framework, this new record (the newspaper article) can be seen as a pluralisation of the existing one (the Bidjara cave paintings). It is a record created in the continuum that is the story of the Bidjara cave paintings. The original record was pluralised when the photographs of the paintings were published in *The Queenslander*. In the process of pluralisation the record is dis-embedded from its original context, community and meaning. The new record gained additional provenance information derived from a society markedly different from the one that created the original record.

The newspaper article ('Prehistoric Aboriginal Art', 1909, p. 29) states that, 'The oldest blacks in the neighbourhood have no knowledge of ever seeing or hearing about these paintings'. When Leann explains why this is inaccurate she does so by explaining the societal provenance, that is, both the Bidjara and non-Indigenous ways of knowing, that brought this article to bear. Accurate appraisal and interpretation of this record require an understanding of the multiple provenances of the record. Choosing to explain the record with just one of those provenances would significantly impact the understanding of the record.

Perhaps the strongest concordance between the green ribbon and blue ribbon stories and the records' continuum model is the notion of non-linear storying. This conceptual framework can easily be mistaken as a linear temporal framework – after all the ribbons themselves are literal lines – but it is important to remember that Aboriginal and Torres Strait Islander histories are non-linear and often cyclical in nature, and in this regard, the green ribbon and blue ribbon stories' framework resembles the records' continuum model. It is sobering to think that the green ribbon has looped tens of thousands of times through the records' continuum as each oral record is told and retold, and applied and reapplied to each Aboriginal or Torres Strait Islander generation to maintain our cultures and care for our Traditional Countries. This act of bringing Traditional Knowledge into contemporary discourse is an act of pluralisation.

In comparison to green ribbon stories, the blue ribbon stories have had a relatively brief existence in the Australian continent's history, but owing to the preference for colonial nation-building narratives, and the western archival practice of prioritising text-based records created by colonists, the blue ribbon stories have been repeatedly and strategically pluralised in the short period since invasion. As a result, blue ribbon stories have dominated our understanding of this continent's history since invasion. For the past 250 or so years, the blue ribbon story has also pluralised repeatedly, sometimes in conjunction with the green ribbon story, but mostly not.

In her book 'We come with this place' Gudanji/Wakaja,[45] author Debra Dank relates a story that demonstrates the long cyclical nature of Indigenous recordkeeping via living archives on Country. Dank tells the story of her family being led on a walk on their Traditional Country by their Aunty. The Aunty stops at a circle of cycads where she picks the strongest looking nuts from the cycad plants and passes them to the children. She then asks the children to use their feet to create a hole in which to plant the seed they have been given. As the children do this, their aunty explains that each of the existing cycads has been planted in the same way by their ancestors. The Aunt, a woman in her eighties, points to an existing cycad and says, 'This one here… I put with my grandmother. I was a young girl'. and pointing at another larger cycad, 'That one, my mother put with her grandmother. That big one there, grandmother's grandmother put there when she was a little one with her granny'.[46] The green ribbon story of that place is one of intentional land management and small scale agriculture to support food security. When we consider the cycad grove as a records' continuum, we see each plant is a record of both a person and a cultural practice, but also a pluralisation of the stories of each previous cycad planting event. As McKemmish et al.[47] put it, 'Records are also embodied in people and embedded in Country'. The blue ribbon story, one can easily imagine, is seeing a cluster of cycads and assuming that they had occurred there by chance – that the Traditional Owners' existence is parallel to, but inconsequential to that of the natural environment.

The green ribbon and blue ribbon stories need not be diametrically opposed to each other but can remind us that there are multiple influences on any record. Tom Nesmith[48] and Chris Hurley[49] argue that all records have multiple provenances, and that these multiple provenances should be considered as part of any record appraisal, description and interpretation. Nesmith states that all records have societal provenance and all provenance has societal dimensions. People create records for social purposes according to their understanding of society and their place in it.[50] The record creator's circumstances influence what they perceive as trustworthy, authentic, reliable and what they consider worth remembering or forgetting.[51] It also influences where the record creator gathers their information from, who they have access to and who they see as a trustworthy source. The green ribbon and blue ribbon stories are two provenance channels specific to colonised nations that should always be considered when appraising, describing and interpreting records. In the case of the 1909 *Queenslander* article about the Bidjara cave paintings, the societal provenance of the article dramatically affects the interpretation of the record. By using the green ribbon and blue ribbon stories framework, we are perhaps not decolonising the records, but we are reaffirming Indigenous sovereignty in all records that relate to Traditional Countries in so-called Australia. As Hurley asserts, integrating these multiple provenances into the record does not detract from it, but enriches it.[52]

The application of the green ribbon and blue ribbon stories' conceptual framework to archival praxis is particularly relevant at this point in Queensland and Australia's history when truth-telling is seen as a key component of the Treaty process.[53] While postmodern theory precludes the possibility of knowing anything as an absolute truth, the green ribbon and blue ribbon stories' conceptual framework consistently applied to archival records used in truth telling can assist in the interpretation of those records to ensure that both Indigenous and non-Indigenous worldviews and lived experiences contribute to understanding shared histories.

Conclusion

This journal article introduces the green ribbon and blue ribbon stories' conceptual framework that has been developed from an Indigenous, specifically Bidjara worldview. This conceptual framework, developed by Bidjara woman Leann Wilson, is drawn from her Bidjara ways of being and knowing. The green ribbon and blue ribbon stories' conceptual framework is shared through this publication in the hope that others will find it useful for appraising and interpreting records. This article details the special consideration given to the appropriate ways for the conceptual framework to be used and how to protect the IP and cultural authority of Leann as the developer of the conceptual framework and her family as holders and teachers of the underpinning Bidjara knowledge. In discussing the IP and cultural authority considerations for the green ribbon and blue ribbon stories, we have introduced the use of TK Notices to academic publishing and demonstrated how researchers can make public disclosures of Indigenous Knowledge in their work. The green ribbon and blue ribbon stories' conceptual framework has synergies with existing archival theoretical and conceptual frameworks such as the records' continuum model, societal provenance and parallel provenance. This conceptual framework differs in that it has been developed from an Indigenous worldview by a lay-user of archives. This article's three distinct sections (introducing the green ribbon and blue ribbon stories; giving clear guidelines for its use and attribution and relating the green ribbon and blue ribbon stories' conceptual framework to archival appraisal and interpretation) provide the reader with a new tool for archival appraisal and interpretation, as well as guidance for how to use that tool. This article argues that in colonial countries at least two provenances, Indigenous (represented by the green ribbon) and non-Indigenous (represented by the blue ribbon) should always be considered when appraising, describing and interpreting archival records.

Acknowledgements

The authors would like to recognise the enduring knowledge authority of the Bidjara people and all First Nations across the Australian continent.

Many thanks to the Local Contexts team for helping us to apply TK Notices for the very first time in an academic publication. Thank you to *Archives and Manuscripts* General Editor, Jessie Lymn for her support and collaboration with the authors and the Local Contexts team.

Conflict of interest

After submitting this article but before receiving the reviewers' comments, Rose Barrowcliffe was invited to become the 2023–2024 Global Co-Chair for the Equity for Indigenous Research and Innovation Coordinating Hub (ENRICH), which is directly involved in supporting the adoption of Local Contexts Labels and Notices.

Notes

1. The Bidjara Nation is located in central-western Queensland, Australia.
2. Unknown. (1909, October 23). Prehistoric Aboriginal Art. *The Queenslander*, p. 29.
3. Terri Janke's (Wuthathi/Meriam) gives several examples in her book True Tracks: Indigenous Cultural and Intellectual Property Principles for Putting Self-Determination into Practice, NewSouth Publishing, Sydney, 2021.
4. Linda Tuhiwai Smith (Ngati Awa and Ngati Porou), Decolonizing Methodologies: Research and Indigenous Peoples, 2nd Revised edition, Zed Books Ltd, London, 2012.
5. Barbara Charbonneau-Dahlen (American Indian Chippewa), 'Symbiotic Allegory as Innovative Indigenous Research Methodology', Advances in Nursing Science, vol. 43, no. 1, 2020, pp. E25–35, doi: 10.1097/ANS.0000000000000257; Maggie Kovach (Saulteaux and Plains Cree), 'Emerging from the Margins: Indigenous Methodologies', in Susan Strega and Leslie Brown (eds.), Research as Resistance, Canadian Scholars' Press, Toronto, pp. 43-64, available at https://books.google.com.au/books?hl=en&lr=&id=4UNVCgAAQBAJ&oi=fnd&pg=PA43&dq=info:eXrWnVM9AscJ:scholar.google.com&ots=WNAfOohRoI&sig=ktYDnDh3E88zakAv34gjGeR-LaI&redir_esc=y#v=onepage&q&f=false, accessed 26 November 2021; Linda Tuhiwai Smith, Decolonizing Methodologies: Research and Indigenous Peoples, 2nd Revised edition, Zed Books Ltd, London, 2012.
6. Stuart Barlo (Yuin), William Edgar Boyd, Alessandro Pelizzon, Shawn Wilson (Opaskwayak Cree), 'Yarning as Protected Space: Relational Accountability in Research', AlterNative: An International Journal of Indigenous Peoples, vol. 16, no. 2, 2020, pp. 90-8, doi: 10.1177/1177180120986151; Dawn Bessarab (Bardi) and Bridget Ng'andu, 'Yarning About Yarning as a Legitimate Method in Indigenous Research', International Journal of Critical Indigenous Studies, vol. 3, no. 1, 2010, pp. 37-50, doi: 10.5204/ijcis.v3i1.57.
7. Stuart Barlo (Yuin), William Edgar Boyd, Alessandro Pelizzon, Shawn Wilson (Opaskwayak Cree); Shawn Wilson.
8. Bindi Bennett (Gamilaraay), 'Australian Social Work: Proposed Guidelines for Articles by Aboriginal and Torres Strait Islander Authors and about Aboriginal and Torres Strait Islander Issues', Australian Social Work, vol. 75, no. 3, 2022, pp. 273–9.
9. Nathan Mudyi Sentance (Wiradjuri), 'Indigenous Referencing Prototype – Non-Indigenous Authored Works', available at https://archivaldecolonist.com/, accessed 7 May 2020; Cameron Gooley, 'Sydney University Library Overhauls How People Use Indigenous Resources', Sydney Morning Herald, June 3 2022, available at https://www.smh.com.au/national/australia-s-oldest-uni-library-overhauls-how-people-use-indigenous-resources-20220530-p5apjm.html, accessed 23 March 2023.
10. UTS, 'APA 7th Referencing Guide', pp. 101–7, available at https://www.uts.edu.au/sites/default/files/article/downloads/UTS%20Interactive%20APA%20guide.pdf, accessed 23 March 2023.
11. James Cook University, First Nations Works, APA (7th Edition) Referencing Guide – Library Guides at James Cook University, available at https://libguides.jcu.edu.au/apa/First-Nations, accessed 23 March 2023.
12. Mark John Lock (Ngiyampaa), Faye McMillan (Wiradjuri), Donald Warne (Oglala Lakota), Bindi Bennett (Gamilaraay), Jacquie Kidd (Ngāpuhi), Naomi Williams (Bkejwanong), Jodie Lea Matire, Paull Worley, Peter Hutten-Czapski, Emily Saurman, Veronica Matthews (Quandamooka), Emma Walke (Bundalung), Dave Edwards (Worimi), Julie Owen (Nurrunga and Ngarrendjeri), Jennifer Brown & Russell Roberts, 'Indigenous Cultural Identity of Research Authors Standard: Research and Reconciliation with Indigenous Peoples in Rural Health Journals', Canadian Journal of Rural Medicine, vol. 27, no. 3, p. 7646, doi: 10.22605/RRH7646.
13. ICIRAS goes beyond requesting that cultural identity is including in authors by-lines, it calls for change at all levels of academic publication by suggesting academic publications: conduct an audit of the status of Indigenous peoples at all levels of their governance, including editorial boards and the various stages of publishing; update the manuscript submission process to include questions about author indigeneity and Indigenous participation in the research; revise author guidelines to acknowledge Indigenous contributions; and, have a public statement on their position on research with Indigenous peoples.
14. Lock et al.
15. Ibid.
16. Rose Barrowcliffe (Butchulla) for National and State Libraries of Australasia, NSLA Contemporary Collections Audit, 2022, available at https://www.nsla.org.au/sites/default/files/2022-05/nsla-indigenous-collections-audit-stage2.pdf, accessed 15 January 2023.

17. The Archives & Manuscripts website gives the following definition of authorship for journal article submissions:
    Each of the manuscript's authors should meet all three of the following criteria: (1) has made a substantial contribution to the design of the study, the collection of the data, or the analysis or interpretation of the data; (2) has drafted the manuscript or helped revise it, shaping its intellectual content; (3) has approved of the submitted manuscript.
    Archives & Manuscripts, 'Authorship', n.d., available at https://publications.archivists.org.au/index.php/asa/authorship, accessed 13 January 2023.
18. Local Contexts, 'Local Contexts Overviews', n.d., available at https://drive.google.com/file/d/1XuqC-sIDruKcH98sK529IrhDZZaTcRDT_/view, accessed 20 December 2022.
19. Martin Nakata (Torres Strait Islander), 'The Cultural Interface', The Australian Journal of Indigenous Education, vol. 36, no.1, 2007, pp. 7–14.
20. Commonwealth of Australia, Copyright Act 1968, 1968, available at https://www.legislation.gov.au/Details/C2019C00042, accessed 16 January 2023.
21. Commonwealth of Australia, Copyright Act – Regulations – Statutory Rules 1969 No. 65, available at https://parlinfo.aph.gov.au/parlInfo/search/display/display.w3p;query=Id%3A%22publications%2Ftabledpapers%2FHSTP0459_1969%22;src1=sm1, 1969, accessed 16 January 2023; and Commonwealth of Australia, Copyright (International Protection) Regulations 1969, 1969, available at http://classic.austlii.edu.au/au/legis/cth/consol_reg/cpr1969506/, accessed 16 January 2023.
22. Commonwealth of Australia, Short Guide to Copyright, 2016, available at https://www.infrastructure.gov.au/sites/default/files/short_guide_to_copyright.pdf, accessed 17 January 2023.
23. Copyright Council of Australia, Introduction to Copyright in Australia, 2022, available at https://www.copyright.org.au/browse/book/ACC-An-Introduction-to-Copyright-in-Australia-INFO010/, accessed 16 January 2023.
24. Commonwealth of Australia, 1968.
25. Terri Janke explores the conflicts between Indigenous Knowledge ownership and IP law extensively in her work and research. See Terri Janke, True Tracks, New South Publishing, Sydney, 2021.
26. Cases where Indigenous Knowledge became the IP of academics are plentiful. For example, anthropologist Margaret Lawie's 1970 book 'Myths and Legends of the Torres Strait' made Lawrie the copyright owner of oral histories and stories from across the Torres Strait.
27. Copyright Council of Australia, 2022.
28. Madhavi Sunder, 'The Invention of Traditional Knowledge', Law and Contemporary Problems, vol. 70, no. 2, 2007, pp. 97–124.
29. James Boyle, Shamans, Software, and Spleens: Law and the Construction of the Information Society, Harvard University Press, Cambridge, USA and London, England, 1996.
30. Ibid.
31. Sunder.
32. Ibid., p. 101.
33. World Intellectual Property Organization, Intellectual Property and Traditional Knowledge, 2006, available at https://www.wipo.int/edocs/pubdocs/en/tk/920/wipo_pub_920.pdf, accessed 20 January 2023.
34. For more information on Local Contexts labels https://localcontexts.org, accessed 15 January 2023.
35. Jane Anderson, 'Local Contexts', available at https://vimeo.com/622861354, accessed 4 October 2021, 00:00:43.
36. Ibid., 00:01:19.
37. Maui Hudson (Whakatōhea), 'Local Contexts', available at https://vimeo.com/622861354, accessed 4 October 2021, 00:06:52.
38. Stephani Russo Carroll, Ibrahim Garba, Oscar L Figueroa-Rodríguez, Jarita Holbrook, Raymond Lovett, Simeon Materechera, Mark Parsons, Kay Raseroka, Desi Rodriguez-Lonebear, Robyn Rowe, Rodrigo Sara, Jennifer D Walker, Jane Anderson and Maui Hudson, 'The CARE Principles for Indigenous Data Governance', Data Science Journal, vol. 19, no. 1, 2020, p. 43, doi: 10.5334/dsj-2020-043.
39. Local Contexts, 'Local Contexts Overviews', n.d., available at https://drive.google.com/file/d/1XuqC-sIDruKcH98sK529IrhDZZaTcRDT_/view, accessed 20 December 2022.
40. Ibid.; Kimberley Christen, 'Tribal Archives, Traditional Knowledge, and Local Contexts: Why the "S" Matters', Journal of Western Archives, vol. 6, no. 1, 2015, pp. 1–19.
41. Local Contexts, 'Local Contexts', available at https://vimeo.com/622861354, accessed 4 October 2021.

42. Tom Nesmith, 'Reopening Archives: Bringing New Contextualities into Archival Theory and Practice', Archivaria, vol. 60, ed. Fall 2005, 2005, pp. 259–74; Tom Nesmith, 'The Concept of Societal Provenance and Records of Nineteenth-Century Aboriginal-European Relations in Western Canada: Implications for Archival Theory and Practice', Archival Science, vol. 6, nos. 3–4, 2006, pp. 351–60, doi: 10.1007/S10502-007-9043-9/FIGURES/3.
43. Chris Hurley, 'Parallel Provenance: (1) What, If Anything, Is Archival Description?', Archives and Manuscripts, vol. 33, no. 1, 2005a, pp. 110–43, doi: 10.3316/ielapa.200601141; Chris Hurley, 'Parallel Provenance (If These Are Your Records, Where Are Your Stories?)', 2005b; Chris Hurley, 'Parallel Provenance Part 2: When Something Is Not Related to Everything Else', Archives and Manuscripts, vol. 33, no. 2, pp. 52–91, doi: 10.3316/ielapa.200601141.
44. Joanne Evans, Sue McKemmish and Greg Rolan, 'Crticial Approaches to Archiving and Recordkeeping in the Continuum', Journal of Critical Library and Information Studies, vol. 1, no. 2, 2017, pp. 122–60, doi: 10.24242/jclis.v1i2.35; Sue McKemmish, Frank Upward and Barbara Reed, 'Records Continuum Model', in Marcia J Bates and Mary Niles Maack (eds.), Encyclopedia of Library and Information Sciences, 3rd edition, CRC Press, Boca Raton, 2009, pp. 4447–59, doi: 10.1081/E-ELIS3-120043719; Barbara Reed, 'Reading the Records Continuum: Interpretations and Explorations', Archives and Manuscripts, vol. 33, no. 1, 2005, pp. 18–43, doi: 10.3316/ielapa.200601137; Frank Upward, 'Structuring the Records Continuum Part One: Post-Custodial Principles and Properties', Archives and Manuscripts, vol. 24, no. 2, 1996, pp. 268–85; Frank Upward, 'Structuring the Records Continuum Part Two: Structuration Theory and Recordkeeping', Archives and Manuscripts, vol. 25, no. 1, 1997, pp. 10–35, doi: 10.3316/ielapa.980100005.
45. Debra Dank (Gudanji/Wakaja), We Come with this Place, Echo Publishing, London, 2022.
46. Ibid., p. 243.
47. Sue McKemmish, Tom Chandler and Shannon Faulkhead (Koorie), 'Imagine: A Living Archive of People and Place "Somewhere beyond Custody"', Archival Science, vol. 19, no. 3, 2019, pp. 281–301, doi: 10.1007/s10502-019-09320-0.
48. Tom Nesmith, 'Reopening Archives: Bringing New Contextualities into Archival Theory and Practice', Archivaria, vol. 60, Fall 2005, pp. 259–74; Tom Nesmith, 'The Concept of Societal Provenance and Records of Nineteenth-Century Aboriginal-European Relations in Western Canada: Implications for Archival Theory and Practice', Archival Science, vol. 6, nos. 3–4, 2006, pp. 351–60, doi: 10.1007/S10502-007-9043-9/FIGURES/3.
49. Chris Hurley, 'Parallel Provenance: (1) What, If Anything, Is Archival Description?', Archives and Manuscripts, vol. 33, no. 1, 2005a, pp. 110–43, doi: 10.3316/ielapa.200601141; Chris Hurley, 'Parallel Provenance (If These Are Your Records, Where Are Your Stories?)', 2005b; Hurley, 'Parallel Provenance Part 2', 2005c.
50. Tom Nesmith, 'The Concept of Societal Provenance and Records of Nineteenth-Century Aboriginal-European Relations in Western Canada: Implications for Archival Theory and Practice', Archival Science, vol. 6, no. 3–4, 2006, pp. 351–60, doi: 10.1007/S10502-007-9043-9/FIGURES/3.
51. Ibid., p. 352.
52. Hurley, 2005a.
53. In 2022, the incoming Australian Prime Minister, Anthony Albanese, made a commitment to the Uluru Statement of the Heart and promised a referendum on an Indigenous voice to parliament in his first term as Prime Minister (see Emma Lee, 'Prime Minister Albanese's Victory Speech Brings Hope for First Nations Peoples' Role in Democracy', The Conversation, 22 May 2022, available at https://theconversation.com/prime-minister-albaneses-victory-speech-brings-hope-for-first-nations-peoples-role-in-democracy-183454, accessed 24 March 2023; and Lorena Allam, 'Voice, Treaty, Truth', The Guardian, 22 May 2022, available at https://www.theguardian.com/australia-news/2022/may/22/voice-treaty-truth-what-does-labors-commitment-to-uluru-statement-from-the-heart-mean, accessed 24 March 2023. Also in 2022, the Queensland Government committed to Treaty or Treaties with the First Nations of Queensland. In accepting all the recommendations of the Treaty Advancement Committee, either in part or full, the Queensland Government committed to a truth telling process for the people of Queensland. See Queensland Government, 'Palaszczuk Government Launches the Start of the Formal Path to Treaty', 16 August 2022, available at https://statements.qld.gov.au/statements/95967, accessed 24 March 2023.

ARTICLE

Created, Intended, Articulated and Projected: Four Perceptions of Purpose Around the Archival Document for Expert Users

Sarah Welland*

Library and Information Studies, Open Polytechnic | Te Pūkenga, Lower Hutt, New Zealand

Abstract

This article presents a new model of four perceptions of purpose relating to the archival document in archival organisations. It explains created purpose (it is what it is), intended purpose (it is what the creating or host organisation attests it as), articulated purpose (it is what the archival organisation presents it as) and projected purpose (it is what the user signifies it as) and outlines why an understanding of these may be useful for expert users in research. The article also references and supports discourse covering the conceptualisation and critical reflection of users and their interaction with the archival document.

Keywords: *Archival document; Archival practice; Expert users; Perceptions of archives; Purpose of archives.*

User perceptions around the different purposes of the archival document are not much discussed in archival literature. This article helps to address this by discussing a new model that formulates four perceptions of purpose as they relate to the archival document in an archival organisation. It explains each purpose and outlines why an understanding of each may provide helpful insight for highly proficient and informed (expert) users who interact with the archival document as part of their research. The four perceptions of purpose discussed are *created purpose* (the archival document is perceived as evidence of an initial task), *intended purpose* (the archival document is perceived as evidence of actions or decisions), *articulated purpose* (the archival document is perceived as evidence of a curated account), and *projected purpose* (the archival document is perceived as evidence of repurposed narrative). It is the intention of the article to also support discourse relating to the conceptualisation and critical reflection of the archival document's creation, (re)use and management over time, as well as discussion concerning expert users' reflective practices around the archival document.

The four perceptions of purpose model is based on critical analysis of archival processes and user engagement, published literature, and traditional notions of archiving and record-keeping epistemology. It is also influenced by the records continuum theory[1] in terms of its consideration

*Correspondence: Sarah Welland, Email: Sarah.welland@openpolytechnic.ac.nz

of the plurality of the archival document as evidence of a transaction, a concatenated record, and a (re)presented item. Within the article, each perception of purpose is closely influenced by the places the archival document has been created, amended, and managed as a record, and selected, described and managed as an archive. It presumes established forms of archival arrangement within the archival organisation holding the archival document; particularly those forms to do with custody[2] and 'the traditional European theory of arrangement as constituted by the principles of respect des fonds and respect for original order'.[3] However, while the article recognises that the archival document is evidence of the direct relationship between record and event, it also accepts that the record can serve as a narrative,[4] interpreted as 'a sign, a signifier, a meditated and ever-changing construction'.[5] Finally, the article presumes that the expert user takes an active role in seeking out and addressing the various purpose-related questions and issues discovered in their research involving archival documents.

With these assumptions in mind, the article aims to contribute to discussion and 'on-going critical interpretation'[6] around the user and the archival document. Methodologically, it uses a review of literature to create a form of think piece that discusses how an awareness of four different ways of archival document can be perceived. This can help expert users identify many of the diverse influences affecting the presentation of the archival document covers a range of topics. These include 'small histories' of individual lives;[7] exclusion and misrepresentation;[8] the archivist-historian relationship;[9] business history;[10] ethnographic analysis;[11] and feeling, emotion and affect.[12] However, most discourse does not seem to include discussion relating to users and how they perceive the purposes of the archives they use.[13]

Identifying the influences affecting their interaction with the archival document can help users such as expert users determine why the archival document 'is presented the way it is' by the archival organisation, in turn informing how expert users critique or champion the archival document to potentially 'transformative affect'.[14] These influences can support users' ability to address questions such as 'why does the archival organisation describe it this way? Why is access restricted?' 'Why are there gaps?' and to start to identify some of the agendas operating around the archival organisation itself.[15] The answers that are obtained can help expert users to understand the different reasons why an archival document was created, used, and kept regardless of their own epistemological lens. The four perceptions of purpose model can also assist users to gain a better understanding of the archival document as a record, the archival organisation that holds it, and their own reactions to both aspects. This understanding can in turn help expert users to consider whether their interaction with the archival document is affected 'of, by or for' the document's creating or host organisation, 'of, by or for' the archival organisation that manages it, 'of, by or for' the expert user themselves, or a mixture of all three.

Situating terminology

The terms used in this article have the potential to be perceived differently, depending on the reader's own understanding of archives. Archival theory and praxis are not fixed but open to critical review, creating new and ongoing definitions of the archive as an 'epistemic thing'.[16] This results in the archival document being a potential 'nexus of evidence' from which multiple interpretations can be made, based on influences like content, location, description, accessibility, documentation and the epistemological understandings of the user. Therefore, the following definitions have been provided to demarcate the key terms used in this article.

Archival document is defined as a purposefully collected physical or digital record that provides evidence and/or 'tells a story' – one which is intentionally held and managed within an archival organisation (usually as part of a larger collection). This definition is derived from the

Continuum Theory[17] as the theory does not aggregate document, record and archive, allowing the archival document in its 'recordness' to be viewed as (among other things) evidence within the process of recordkeeping.[18] Accepting that evidence as a concept can be questioned,[19] the archival document can still be defined through the traces of its creation, re-creation, use and re-use as a record. While the term 'archival document' may not always reflect the varied nuances around the archival item (particularly oral sources or individuals and communities who are subjects rather than creators), it provides a useful confinement of scope when it comes to the discussion of the four perceptions of purpose in this article, as the more generic term 'archive' can encompass item, group, collection, place, concept, or movement.

Expert user is used to determine the levels of knowledge and experience a user may need to fully apply the four perceptions of purpose to an archival document. Typically, an expert user will be an experienced and knowledgeable researcher who is invested in their research topic[20] and who creates recognised authoritative outputs such as articles, books, websites and reports. Expert users are often 'self-conscious and politically-attuned users of the archive'[21] who are actively engaged in the process of conceptualisation and critical reflection around the archival document and how they are using it. Expert users may be historians, professional researchers or academics, or else non-professionals with extensive research and/or life experience.

Archival organisation is used to include the different communities, repositories or even individuals that purposely maintain archival documents. For repositories, these may be mainstream, alternative, physical or virtual. It is expected that examples of archival organisations are validated by some 'level of legitimation or authorisation'[22] as well as by evidence of ongoing stewardship.[23] This allows them to be viewed by users as an authentic and reliable place where archival documents are managed, regardless of other influences and agendas.

Creating organisation and *host organisation* are used to define the organisations that caused the archival document to be (among other things) created, received, used, re-used, amended, described, organised and stored as a record prior to it being archived. These organisations can include individuals, groups, communities, and agencies that are private, public, or voluntary. Often the creating organisation and the host organisation are the same.

Presented is the word used to cover the various custodial processes and services carried out by the archival organisation as they make the archival document available to users. This includes selection, listing, cataloguing, boxing, shelving and the creation of metadata, information systems and finding aids. It can also include guidelines and rules around donorship, collaboration participation, access and use, provision of working spaces, and exhibition and display.

Interaction is used to summarise the processes involved to create a state where the user can critically reflect,[24] conceptualise and/or 'make meaning' in relation to the archival documents they use within an archival organisation. Interaction includes the user's emotional responses to the archival document itself,[25] and encompasses the notion of information use behaviour and the mental acts involved in finding, accessing, and engaging with the archival document within an archival organisation, interpreting it, and 'incorporating the information found into the person's existing knowledge base'.[26] This may involve reflective practices such as 'awareness of constructive and literary aspect, the specific characteristics of the sources, and the narratives built in archives and documents as well as the narratives derived from them'.[27]

Representing the four perceptions of purpose

The four perceptions of purpose that can be applied to an archival document within an archival organisation are represented in the model below (see Figure 1). Each perception of purpose is then discussed in turn.

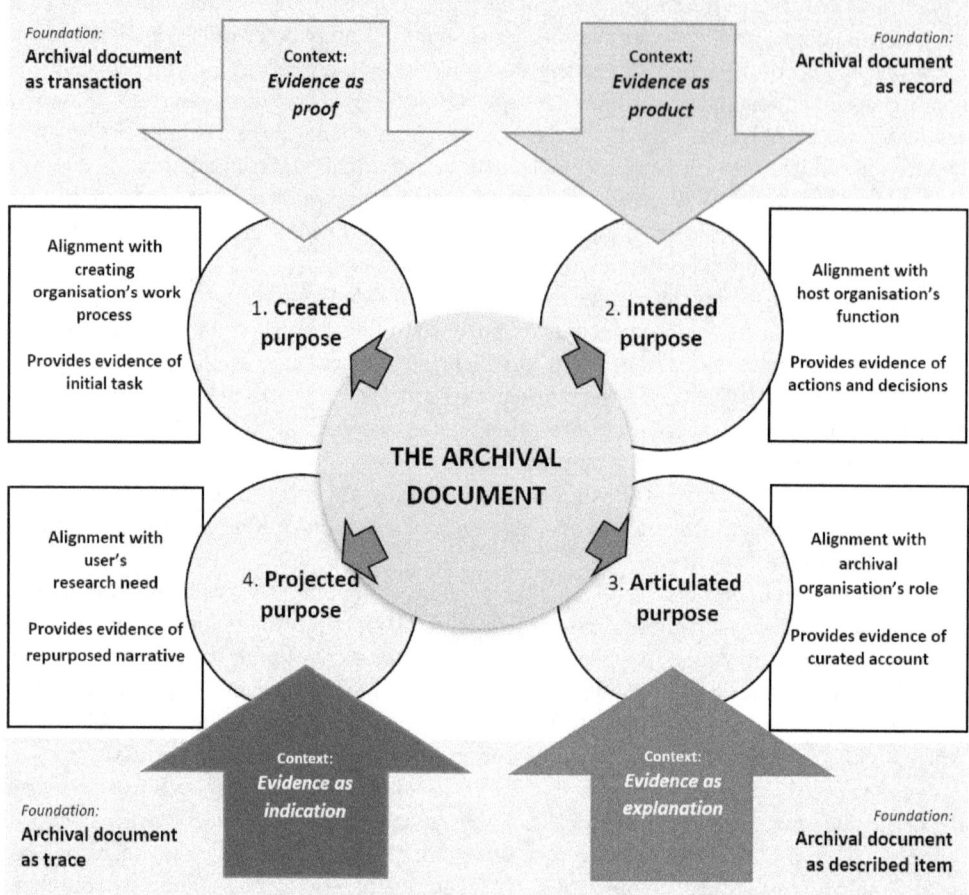

Figure 1. Four perceptions of purpose that can be applied to the archival document within an archival organisation.

Created purpose

Created purpose invites the user into the organisational perspective, but its scope is narrow due to the limited nature of the original intent behind the creation of the 'source' record. Through the lens of created purpose, the archival document is viewed as a transactional record – one that is often created as accepted proof of a minor and/or repeated transaction that has occurred within prescribed and pre-set tasks or processes.[28] For example, a financial transaction resulting as a receipt, or a legal transaction as a signed document. A useful foundational explanation of this concept is 'archival documents first and foremost provide evidence of the transactions of which they are a part – from this they derive their meanings and informational value'.[29] The term 'transaction' is not always easy to define from a recordkeeping perspective, although it is often used to explain the concept of record and its evidential purpose in the sense of 'transacting business of any kind, whether by governments, businesses, community organisations or private individuals'.[30] This usually occurs 'in the normal course of… business activity'.[31]

By presenting the archival document as evidence of a transaction, the perception of created purpose raises the user's awareness of the value of the archival document in its contextual integrity as a 'small something', regardless of greater meanings that can be applied to it. That is, it is what it is. This then bids the question: *why did the creating organisation generate it this way?* hopefully producing answers that demonstrate an understanding that something happened because evidence exists that a transaction occurred – a receipt was produced, or a document was signed.

This more concentrated insight into the transactions that make up the creating organisation's systems and processes can be a useful way of interpreting its larger workings. For instance, it may help an expert user to find out more about the original 'place'[32] of creation and the tasks, systems and processes that brought about the transaction (and evidence of it). Such knowledge can also help the expert user to confirm the existence of common incidences within the day-to-day business of an organisation and the 'experience of the parties to the transaction',[33] helping them to better judge the meaning of any deviations or aberrations. For example, finding an unsigned document within a group of signed ones may help to establish whether this occurred because of human error, a deliberate action, or unfinished business.

Intended purpose

Intended purpose, like created purpose, invites the user into the organisational perspective, but the scope is broader, covering the various organisational intentions behind the creation and use of the archival document as a record. That is, via the lens of intended purpose, the 'recordness' of the archival document is established through the existing evidence of its business activity, its role as an information asset, and its authenticity, reliability, integrity and useability over time.[34] As a concept, intended purpose helps to identify content that can give an account of what happened to an archival document before it was processed as 'an archive'.[35]

As intended purpose is perceived this way, the archival document can be explained as one of many records the creating or host organisation used within the context of a function or activity. Intended purpose considers the archival document '*as* a record' rather than '*from* a record', understanding it as a form of mediated 'evidence as product' within a structured organisational context. This in turn raises the question: *why did the creating organisation represent it this way?* providing opportunity to consider the organisation's original attestation of intentions and decision-making in the creation of the archival document. It also invites consideration of the contemporary processes affecting the conscious formation and official collection of records as products and assets, and deliberation around the contemporaneous infrastructures[36] and record-keeping systems impacting the formation and use of the archival document as a record. Duff and Harris claim that 'information about record-keeping systems, functions, and activities… plays an essential role in understanding the deeper contextual meaning of records',[37] something that Trace attributes to the fact that they are 'causally affecting' the processes they measure.[38] This information may help expert users establish how creating and host organisations presented and mediated themselves through their classification structures and/or metadata, as well as identify existing links between the archival document and others within the same aggregates such as archival fonds or archival series. This information can also assist expert users to establish how an archival document 'was presented' in the classification structures that noted its existence as a record and ascertain the archival document's intended purpose and meaning in relation to other, existing, archival documents that are contextually related to it. For example, to determine whether modifications or corrections to schemes or proposals in archival documents indicate competing viewpoints, human error, external influences or changing organisational priorities.

A perception of intended purpose can therefore help to establish the organisational intent behind the creation of the archival document as a record (as implied through associated classification structures and metadata), so it can be compared with the documented result (as demonstrated through the content and metadata of the record itself). This perception also provides opportunities for insight into the creating and host organisations' own tacit (unspoken and/or assumed) and explicit (acknowledged and/or stated) knowledge relating to its narratives and experiences (that is, its 'doings, sayings and relatings').[39] This provides another way of seeing the evidence of the intent behind organisational functions or activities in addition to the evidence of the functions or activities themselves. For example, a contract may provide just as much evidence of a need to demonstrate success as evidence that the contract was successfully completed.

Articulated purpose

Articulated purpose again invites the user into the organisational perspective, but this is focused on the archival organisation responsible for the archival document. It considers how the archival organisation presents and describes the archival document as a record, and whether these are affected by the organisation's custodial viewpoint.[40] An archival organisation's custodial viewpoint varies considerably from archival organisation to archival organisation.[41] This is because it is based on the archival organisation's own understanding of its identity in terms of role, place, purpose, functions, traditions, languages and cultures, and its expressions of each of these aspects in various physical, situational, political, emotional, interventional or other ways.[42]

Through the lens of articulated purpose, an expert user can consider how access tools used within the archival organisation (such as shelving, boxing, metadata, indexes, descriptions and links) display, describe, explain and contextualise the archival document on behalf of the creating and host organisations who were responsible for it as a record, and the people who are represented by these organisations. This includes not only capacity to 'protect and preserve records'[43] but also to 'legitimize and sanctify certain documents while negating and destroying others; and provide access to selected sources while controlling the researchers and conditions under which they may examine the archival record'.[44]

While most archival organisations apply common archival principles such as provenance and original order to give 'archives their context and structure',[45] these principles are expressed differently from organisation to organisation. Being aware of why the archival document is described and presented the way it is by the archival organisation can help expert users to usefully question the archival organisation's descriptions around it in light of various drivers such as the organisation's purpose (we are created to collect these things), aims (we hope to achieve these things), resources (we have the money to do these things), personnel (we have these people to do these things), underlying methodology (we do things this way), and prescribed audience (we do things for these groups of people). Combined with an awareness of intended purpose, an expert user can better understand the fullness of the collection in which the archival document sits and the archival organisation's own custodial approach, helping them to determine aspects such as who 'owns' the archival document, whether it has a full description or is 'divorced' from the context of its creation,[46] whether there is a 'misleading impression of completeness'[47] or it exists as part of an 'archival diaspora' divided across institutions.[48]

The different services around the acquisition and management of the archival document (notably, transfer/donation, selection/appraisal, arrangement and description) can also be reviewed through the lens of articulated purpose. These services can be seen as another expression of the archival organisation's abstract conceptualisations around its perceived identity, resulting in an operating environment that is formed as much by the organisation's perceptions of its place and purpose as it is by available resources. For example, a small community-created archives may provide services that focus on stewardship and 'facilitating community access',[49] while a national archives may present services that fit their perceived role as guardian and 'former of national identity'.[50] Consequently, an awareness of articulated purpose can result in the question: *why did the archival organisation explain it this way?* helping users to identify the reasons why the archival organisation presents the archival document the way it does.

An awareness of articulated purpose can also help expert users establish how arrangement and description practices are explained to the user by the archival organisation, since 'numerous tacit narratives are hidden in the acts of categorization, codification and labelling'.[51] One way to ascertain this is through the role of the archivist.[52] Archivists can be seen as the 'principal actor in defining, choosing, and constructing the archive *that remains*, and then in representing and presenting that surviving archival trace to researchers'.[53] An understanding of articulated purpose can help the expert user to better explain the role of the archivist in relation to the representation of the archival document by the archival organisation.

Projected purpose
A perception of *projected purpose* can be considered broadly, moving away from the organisational perspective and focusing on the variety of unbounded understandings or new imaginings that can occur out of the user's interaction with the archival document. An expert user may use the archival document as trace or partial evidence to indicate the existence of larger issues, hidden stories, or told or untold narratives, based on their own philosophical, social or critical stance and their levels of experience, reflexive practice and domain knowledge.[54]

Through the lens of projected purpose, the expert user can be invited to consider how their own research methodologies, epistemological strategies, recognised subjectivities and confirmation biases match the indications they find within the 'constrained evidence' of the archival document and its subsequent representation by the archival organisation. This invitation creates opportunities for the expert user to consider the narratives they have constructed around the archival document and address the question: *why do I 'see' the archival document this way?* It helps the expert user to decide what the archival document signifies for them in terms of which parts of the archival document's 'presented story' they will accept, which they will ignore, and what any discovered gaps or ambiguities may mean for their research.

In relation to the other three perceptions of purpose (created, intended and articulated), a perception of projected purpose can also provide opportunities for the expert user to reflect on how far the archival document can be relied on to provide evidence in areas it was never created to provide evidence for. For example, they may need to 'acknowledge that things that at first seem relevant may later prove to be irrelevant, and that different people will form different judgments about what is relevant to a given issue'.[55] This, however, still needs to be balanced with the acknowledgement that the archival document is still 'archival' in that it represents some facet of truth, even if it's just its ability to be a reliable representation of what happened[56] as a form of 'socially constructed and maintained entity',[57] or else a reliable perception of it.

Four possible benefits of understanding the four perceptions of purpose

The rest of this article summarises four possible benefits that may come out of an expert user's understanding of the four perceptions of purpose, collectively referred to from this point as 'purpose knowledge'. Purpose knowledge can aid understanding of the archival organisation's influence on the archival document, facilitate the identification of gaps in archival understanding that may bias or hinder research, assist with identifying the validity of any 'purpose projection', and support research around the user's interaction with the archival document.

Purpose knowledge can aid understanding of the archival organisation's influence on the archival document
Purpose knowledge can help users to better understand the archival organisation's influence on the archival document, particularly around selection description and presentation. Decker, a business historian, says that 'each organizational archive needs to be understood on its own terms' when used for research[58] and others have similar views.[59] As a result, users need to understand 'all significant interventions by the archives itself in the history of the record',[60] both social and technical.[61] Purpose knowledge can help users identify significant interventions to the archival document by aiding the identification of classification systems, processes of use and re-use, and rules around ownership,

provenance, destruction and transfer. This in turn can help them to gain an awareness of the different subjectivities around the perceived value of the document as presented by the metadata and descriptive information, as 'notions of value are always contextual'.[62] It can also help them to identify possible (positive or negative) assumption or bias in the selection, description and presentation of the archival document and likely reasons for these. For instance, identification may help the expert user determine whether assumption or bias stems from organisational collection mandates or forms of community representation, or unrecognised colonial thinking or less than ideal 'temporary' descriptions from 20th century finding aids. Alternatively, purpose knowledge can help the expert user identify instances of 'inclusive description',[63] where the archival organisation acknowledges descriptive tensions around how the archival document was and is represented.

This ability to identify evidence of assumption or bias (and how this is addressed by the archival organisation) can help the expert user become more aware of other influences on the archival document as well. Influences include the level by which the archival evidence is constrained through the archival organisation's selection, positioning and description of the archival document, the portrayal of original authors[64] and subject matter, the agenda displayed in the archival organisation's custodial practices[65] or the role of the archivist in determining access.[66] There may also be influences outside of the archival organisation's control, such as 'the personal agenda of visitors and users and the wider economic and social contexts within which the institution operates'.[67] Identifying evidence of assumption or bias can create a greater awareness of the potential range of 'custodial contradictions'[68] in relation to an archival organisation's stewardship practices, particularly those around 'positionality, subjectivity and representation'.[69] This can help the expert user to usefully question their own reaction to the archival organisation as a place and whether they see it as a 'safe space in which to explore...feelings and histories'[70] with archivists who mitigate 'the injustice documented by the records'[71] or a location that projects 'epistemic violence'[72] with archivists perpetuating 'endemic bias'.[73] Regardless of the reaction, greater awareness of assumption or bias within the archival organisation can help the expert user to understand how the archival organisation considers and presents the 'human in the record'[74] and how it may intentionally or unintentionally restrict access to people who live or understand differently.

Purpose knowledge can facilitate the identification of gaps in archival understanding that may bias or hinder research

While the notion of archival context is embedded in archival principles and variously discussed in archival discourse[75], the tangle of context, content and meaning influencing the archival document within an archival organisation can still be a 'foreign country' to many users.[76] This can increase the methodological, conceptual and practical 'divides and disconnects' that have traditionally existed between historians and archivists.[77] Purpose knowledge can help users to address some of their potential gaps around archival knowledge and ask, '*how do I perceive the archival document contextually?*' This can help them to further explore the organisational context and associated subjectivities[78] that influenced its original meaning as a record while still being aware that subsequent archival selection, organisation and description can fall somewhere between 'objective science' and 'subjective response'.[79]

Yakel and Torres[80] state there are three distinct forms of knowledge required to work effectively with primary sources: domain knowledge (knowledge of the research subject), artefactual literacy ('the ability to interpret records and assess their value as evidence'), and archival intelligence (knowledge of 'archival principles, practices, and institutions'). However, history as a discipline 'does not have a consensual way to investigate and write about what happened'[81] and many expert users can 'muddle through with a variety of individual strategies'[82] when researching large amounts of archival material. For expert users, in-depth understanding of the organisations, processes, systems and people involved in the history of the archival document and its cultivation[83] or co-creation[84] by the archival organisation can result in greater understanding of the various meanings that can be gained from it. For instance, it can help to identify the custodial, legal, political and social reasons why the archival document is represented the way it is by the archival organisation and the levels of its 'mediated nature'.[85] It can also help identify the impacts of different people (such as creator, curator, stakeholder and user) had on the archival document in terms of why it was selected and how it was described.

Purpose knowledge can also aid the further development of a user's artefactual literacy and archival intelligence, helping the user to identify potential gaps or bias in content, collection, or cataloguing (such as evidence of unrecognised colonial thinking in archival descriptions) that may cause misunderstanding or feelings of exclusion for some user groups. Purpose knowledge can also help the expert user to establish what these issues may mean in relation to their research. For instance, whether issues were caused by poor recordkeeping practice or systemic bias from the organisations who created or hosted the archival document as a record, or because these organisations considered the content out of scope.

Purpose knowledge helps to assist with identifying the validity of tacit narratives and new imaginings
Research involving archives and discussion of tacit narratives and new imaginings can often consider the interaction between user and archival document.[86] This can open opportunities for exploring related topics such as access, diversity, inspiration, inclusion or participation[87] as well as silences and traces:[88] 'there must be a reckoning with more than evidence of what is past... there is also story, there is imagination and there is future'.[89] However, discussion of tacit narratives and new imaginings involving the archival document still needs to be balanced with the purposes and concerns[90] set around the archival document as a record. This is so users out of their own 'cognitive individualism'[91] don't move past consideration of 'what it may have been' and 'what it could mean for us now' to 'what we want it to mean, regardless'. This is particularly applicable when interacting with archival documents that present a 'profound paradox' in that they can both 'maintain a repressive regime and... hold that regime accountable'[92] (for example, records of state care or land records). Purpose knowledge can help expert users reflect on whether their research with the archival document addresses the document's created and intended purposes or overlooks these purposes in the need to prove other points.

An awareness of purpose knowledge can also help expert users to become more aware of the different areas where they may need to judicially reconstruct meaning around archival documents, transparently describe the known and unknown, and voice any assumptions and known bias in their research.[93] It may also help the expert user to demonstrate awareness of archival gaps such as 'missing links, both literal and figurative'[94] within holdings metadata and finding aids. These aspects can help expert users to keep in mind the processes employed by more traditional archival praxis, the 'implied explicitness' that can come from associated arrangement and description, and the archival document's perceived levels of 'documentary truthfulness'[95] because of these two influences. For instance, by being aware that when reading through lists of selected holdings that often much more was destroyed than kept, and that 'all archival collections are compendia of silences'.[96] Purpose knowledge can therefore aid understanding of the connection or disconnection between the archival document and its intended and actual purposes.

Purpose knowledge can support research around the user's interaction with the archival document
The four perceptions of purpose model and discussion around purpose knowledge can support future research relating to the user's interaction with the archival document. To date, this type of research has been only occasionally discussed in western archival discourse particularly, Yakel and Torres's seminal work on expert users and their information behaviour: *AI: Archival Intelligence and User Expertise*.[97] Other research articles and theses around

users and records and archives exist,[98] but many aspects remain unstudied,[99] or are discussed in non-archival disciplines such as management and organisation studies.[100]

Applied knowledge of the four perceptions of purpose may also be able to contribute to a range of research processes in historical and qualitative research, particularly that involving information use behaviour and/or reflexivity. For example, purpose knowledge could enhance practices around narrative enquiry[101] and historiographical reflexivity[102] as well as ethnography, autobiography and autoethnography.[103] Purpose knowledge can also help in the development of effective search strategies relating to the expert users' own domain knowledge[104] or in the creation of further opportunities to support inclusive practice.[105] Additionally, it can support thinking around qualitative research methods relating to the document and its social affect, and influence thinking around discourse analysis.[106] That is, it could inform questions raised by reflexive discourse analysis around the archival document, particularly, 'how do we know what we think we know about the socio-political role of the discourse and knowledge we produce?'[107]

Conclusion

This article introduces four perceptions of purpose that could be applied to the archival document within an archival organisation, particularly by expert users. These can be summarised as the perception of the archival document's created purpose (it is what it is), the perception of the archival document's intended purpose (it is what the creating or host organisation attests it as), the perception of the archival document's articulated purpose (it is what the archival organisation presents it as), and the perception of the archival document's projected purpose (it is what the user signifies it as).

This model is intended to stimulate further discourse around the user and their interaction with the archival document, such as those involving the different descriptive contexts, gaps and potential meanings surrounding the archival document and the user's own critical reflections around these. Ideally, an awareness of purpose knowledge will help expert users to deepen their understanding of how the archival document is created and used as a record and selected and presented as an archive and use this understanding to inform their own research.

More generally, this article may support archival praxis through a model that encourages clearer communication of notions around western archival practice[108] as well as the better expression of understanding between archival organisations and their expert users in various ways.[109] It may also help archival organisations to explain and contextualise their roles and services around the archival document with greater transparency, especially when faced with the multiple narratives that can be presented of, by or for the individuals, groups and organisations that create, re-create, represent and champion the archival document. For example, by applying specific crowd-sourced user understandings of purpose knowledge to forms of archival description. While the archival document is not always a neutral representation of 'all the past', it does still represent a trace of some of it. Archivists, historians and others are calling for 'new epistemologies'[110] around archival research and praxis that reduce 'the great silence between archivists and historians'[111] when it comes to understanding the archival document as a record. This model will help to support such calls.

Disclosure statements

- No funding was received to assist with the preparation of this manuscript.
- Financial interests: The author declares no financial interests.
- Competing interests: The author is a lecturer at Open Polytechnic | Te Pūkenga and has written for this institution for educational purposes.

Acknowledgements

Thank you to Dr Amanda Cossham, Dr Karin Speedy and Dr Andrew Dickson for their encouragement and support.

ORCID

Sarah Welland

End notes

1. See for example, Joanne Evans, Sue McKemmish, and Greg Rolan, 'Critical Approaches to Archiving and Recordkeeping in the Continuum', Journal of Critical Library and Information Studies, vol. 1, no. 2, 2017, pp. 1–38, doi: 10.24242/jclis.v1i2.35; Sue McKemmish, 'Recordkeeping in the Continuum: An Australian Tradition', in Anne Gilliland, Sue McKemmish, and Andrew Lau (eds.), Research in The Archival Multiverse. Clayton, Victoria: Monash University, 2017, pp. 122–60; Frank Upward, Sue McKemmish, and Barbara Reed, 'Archivists and Changing Social and Information Spaces: A Continuum Approach to Recordkeeping and Archiving in Online Cultures', Archivaria, vol. 72, Fall 2011, pp. 197–237.
2. Jason Lustig, 'Epistemologies of the Archive: Toward a Critique of Archival Reason', Archival Science, vol. 20, no. 1, March 2020, p. 73, doi: 10.1007/s10502-019-09313-z.
3. Heather MacNeil, 'Deciphering and Interpreting an Archival Fonds and Its Parts: A Comparative Analysis of Textual Criticism and the Theory of Archival Arrangement', in Anne Gilliland, Sue McKemmish, and Andrew Lau (eds.), Research in The Archival Multiverse. Clayton, Victoria: Monash University, 2017, p. 162.
4. Jeannette A Bastian, 'Mine, Yours, Ours: Archival Custody from Transaction to Narrative', Archival Science, vol. 21, 2021, p. 27, doi: 10.1007/s10502-020-09341-0.
5. Jennifer Meehan, 'Towards an Archival Concept of Evidence', Master of Archival Studies, University of California, 1997, p. 86, available at http://www.interpares.org/display_file.cfm?doc=ip1_dissemination_thes_meehan_ubc-slais_2003.pdf, accessed 17 January 2023.
6. Joan M Schwartz and Terry Cook, 'Archives, Records, and Power: The Making of Modern Memory', Archival Science, vol. 2, nos. 1–2, March 2002, p. 12, doi: 10.1007/BF02435628.
7. Kate Bagnall and Tim Sherratt, 'Missing Links: Data Stories from the Archive of British Settler Colonial Citizenship', Journal of World History, vol. 32, no. 2, 2021, p. 282, doi: 10.1353/jwh.2021.0025.
8. Michell Caswell, Alda Allina Migoni, Noah Geraci, and Marika Cifor, '"To Be Able to Imagine Otherwise": Community Archives and the Importance of Representation', Archives and Records, vol. 38, no. 1, January 2017, pp. 5–26, doi: 10.1080/23257962.2016.1260445.
9. See for example, Terry Cook, 'The Archive(s) Is a Foreign Country: Historians, Archivists, and the Changing Archival Landscape', The American Archivist, vol. 74, no. 11, Fall / Winter 2011, pp. 600–32, doi: 10.17723/aarc.74.2.xm04573740262424; Alix R Green and Erin Lee, 'From Transaction to Collaboration: Redefining the Academic-Archivist Relationship in Business Collections', Archives & Records, vol. 41, no. 1, Spring 2020, pp. 32–51, doi: 10.1080/23257962.2019.1689109.
10. Stephanie Decker, 'The Silence of the Archives Post Colonialism and the Practice of Historical Reconstruction', Munich Personal RePEc Archive, 2012, available at https://mpra.ub.uni-muenchen.de/37280/1/MPRA_paper_37280.pdf, accessed 17 January 2023.
11. Ciaran B Trace, 'For Love of the Game: An Ethnographic Analysis of Archival Reference Work', Archives & Manuscripts, vol. 34, no. 1, May 2006, pp. 124–43.
12. Hariz Halilovich, 'Re-Imaging and Re-Imagining the Past after "Memoricide": Intimate Archives as Inscribed Memories of the Missing', Archival Science, vol. 16, no. 1, March 2016, pp. 77–92, doi: 10.1007/s10502-015-9258-0.
13. A useful related article in this area is Itza A Carbajal and Michelle Caswell, 'Critical Digital Archives: A Review from Archival Studies', The American Historical Review, vol. 126, no. 3, September 2021, pp. 1102–20, doi: 10.1093/ahr/rhab359. This article focuses on the historian's relationship with digital archives and 'identifies and summarizes seven key themes and corresponding debates about digital records in contemporary archival scholarship: (1) materiality, (2) appraisal, (3) context, (4) use, (5) scale, (6) relationships, and (7) sustainability' (p. 1102).
14. Caswell, Migoni, Geraci, and Cifor.
15. Alix R Green and Erin Lee summarise this well, stating 'the pertinent issue is what agenda governs these decisions'. p. 43.

16. Lustig, p. 68.
17. See for example, Sue McKemmish and Frank Upward, 'The Archival Document: A Submission to the Inquiry into Australia as an Information Society', Archives and Manuscripts, vol. 19, no. 1, 1991, pp. 17–31.
18. See for example, Christopher William Colwell, 'Records Are Practices, Not Artefacts: An Exploration of Recordkeeping in the Australian Government in the Age of Digital Transition and Digital Continuity', Doctoral Thesis, University of Technology, Sydney, 2020, available at https://opus.lib.uts.edu.au/handle/10453/142430, accessed 18 January 2023.
19. Geoffrey Yeo, 'Concepts of Record (1): Evidence, Information, and Persistent Representations', The American Archivist, vol. 70, no. 2, September 2007, p. 325, doi: 10.17723/aarc.70.2.u327764v1036756q.
20. Jonathan Potter and Alexa Hepburn, 'Eight Challenges for Interview Researchers', in Jaber Gubrium, James Holstein, Amir Marvasti, and Karyn McKinney (eds.), The SAGE Handbook of Interview Research: The Complexity of the Craft. 2nd Ed. London: SAGE Publications Inc., 2012, p. 565.
21. Green and Lee, p. 40.
22. Zelmarie Cantillon, Sarah Baker, and Bob Buttigieg, 'Queering the Community Music Archive', Australian Feminist Studies, vol. 32, no. 91–92, April 3, 2017, p. 4, doi: 10.1080/08164649.2017.1357004.
23. Michelle Caswell, Harrison Cole, and Zachary Griffith, 'Images, Silences, and the Archival Record: An Interview with Michelle Caswell', DisClosure: A Journal of Social Theory, vol. 27, July 2018, p. 23.
24. See for example, Amon Barros, Adéle de Toledo Carneiro, and Sergio Wanderley, 'Organizational Archives and Historical Narratives: Practicing Reflexivity in (Re)Constructing the Past from Memories and Silences', Qualitative Research in Organizations and Management: An International Journal, vol. 14, no. 3, 2019, pp. 280–94, doi: 10.1108/QROM-01-2018-1604; Tyler Charlton, 'The Treachery of Archives: Representation, Power, and the Urgency for Self-Reflexivity in Archival Arrangement and Description', The IJournal: Student Journal of the Faculty of Information, vol. 3, no. 1, 2017, pp. 1–8, available at https://theijournal.ca/index.php/ijournal/article/view/28894, accessed 17 January 2022; Stephanie Decker, John Hassard, and Michael Rowlinson, 'Rethinking History and Memory in Organization Studies: The Case for Historiographical Reflexivity', Human Relations, vol. 74, no. 8, August 2021, pp. 1123–55, doi: 10.1177/0018726720927443.
25. Jennifer Douglas, Alexandra Alisauskas, Elizabeth Bassett, Noah Duranseaud, Ted Lee, and Christina Mantey, '"These Are Not Just Pieces of Paper": Acknowledging Grief and Other Emotions in Pursuit of Person-Centered Archives', Archives & Manuscripts, vol. 50, no. 1, July 2022, pp. 5–29, doi: 10.37683/asa.v50.10211.
26. Tom D Wilson, 'Human Information Behavior', Informing Science, vol. 3, no. 2, 2000, p. 50, doi: 10.28945/576.
27. Barros, Carneiro, and Wanderley, p. 281.
28. Sue McKemmish and Frank Upward's article provides useful background in this area.
29. Ibid., p. 19.
30. Ibid.
31. Archives New Zealand, 'Key Definitions – Evidence', July 19, 2022, available at https://www.archives.govt.nz/manage-information/how-to-manage-your-information/implementation/key-definitions, accessed 18 January 2023.
32. Belinda Battley, 'Archives as Places, Places as Archives: Doors to Privilege, Places of Connection or Haunted Sarcophagi of Crumbling Skeletons?', Archival Science, vol. 19, no. 1, 2019, pp. 1–26, doi: 10.1007/s10502-019-09300-4.
33. McKemmish and Upward, p. 21.
34. ISO 15489-1:2016; Geoffrey Yeo, Concepts of Record (1) both provide useful background in this area.
35. See for example Eric Ketelaar, 'Archivistics Research Saving the Profession', The American Archivist, vol. 63, no. 2, September 2000, p. 328, doi: 10.17723/aarc.63.2.0238574511vmv576.
36. Itza A Carbajal and Michelle Caswell summarise this concept as 'architectural, technological, social, epistemological and ethical infrastructures'. p. 1105.
37. Wendy M Duff and Verne Harris, 'Stories and Names: Archival Description as Narrating Records and Constructing Meanings', Archival Science, vol. 2, nos. 3–4, September 2002, p. 271, doi: 10.1007/BF02435625.
38. Ciaran B Trace, 'What Is Recorded Is Never Simply "What Happened": Record Keeping in Modern Organizational Culture', Archival Science, vol. 2, nos. 1–2, March 2002, p. 143, doi: 10.1007/BF02435634.
39. Colwell, p. ix.

40. Wendy M Duff and Verne Harris's article provides useful background, as well as Heather MacNeil, 'Picking Our Text: Archival Description, Authenticity, and the Archivist as Editor', The American Archivist, vol. 68, no. 2, September 2005, pp. 264–78, doi: 10.17723/aarc.68.2.01u65t6435700337.
41. See for example, Michelle Caswell, 'Community-Centered Collecting: Finding Out What Communities Want from Community Archives', Proceedings of the American Society for Information Science and Technology, vol. 51, no. 1, 2014, pp. 1–9, doi: 10.1002/meet.2014.14505101027; Michelle Caswell, Marika Cifor, and Mario H Ramirez, '"To Suddenly Discover Yourself Existing": Uncovering the Impact of Community Archives', The American Archivist, vol. 79, no. 1, June 2016, pp. 56–81, doi: 10.17723/0360-9081.79.1.56; Isto Huvila, 'The Unbearable Lightness of Participating? Revisiting the Discourses of "Participation" in Archival Literature', Journal of Documentation, vol. 71, no. 2, March 2015, pp. 358–86, doi: 10.1108/JD-01-2014-0012; Alexandra Walsham, 'The Social History of the Archive: Record-Keeping in Early Modern Europe', Past & Present, vol. 230, Suppl. 11, 2016, p. 9, doi: 10.1093/pastj/gtw033.
42. See for example Belinda Battley; Judith Etherton,'The Role of Archives in the Perception of Self', Journal of the Society of Archivists, vol. 27, no. 2, October 2006, pp. 227–46, doi: 10.1080/00379810601101301; Riley Linebaugh, 'Reflexivity and Archiving: Reflections on the High Court of Uganda's Archive' Archivoz, October 31, 2018, available at https://www.archivozmagazine.org/en/reflexivity-and-archiving-reflections-on-the-high-court-of-ugandas-archive/, accessed 17 January 2023; Weatherly A Stephan, 'The Platinum Rule Meets the Golden Minimum: Inclusive and Efficient Archival Description of Oral Histories', Journal of Contemporary Archival Studies, vol. 8, no. 11, 2021, pp. 1–16.
43. Randall Jimerson, 'Embracing the Power of Archives', The American Archivist, vol. 69, no. 1, January 2006, p. 20, doi: 10.17723/aarc.69.1.r0p75n2084055418.
44. Ibid.
45. Ketelaar, p. 327.
46. Carbajal and Caswell, p. 1111.
47. MacNeil, p. 273.
48. Ricardo Punzalan, 'Archival Diasporas: A Framework for Understanding the Complexities and Challenges of Dispersed Photographic Collections', The American Archivist, vol. 77, no. 2, December 2014, pp. 326–49, doi: 10.17723/aarc.77.2.729766v886w16007.
49. Sarah Welland, '"Us and Them": Expert and Practitioner Viewpoints on Small New Zealand Community Archives', Information Research, Proceedings of RAILS – Research Applications, Information and Library Studies, 2016: School of Information Management, Victoria University of Wellington, New Zealand, 6–8 December 2016, vol. 22, no. 4, December 2017, available at http://informationr.net/ir/22-4/rails/rails1609.html, accessed 18 January 2023.
50. Michael Karabinos, 'The Role of National Archives in the Creation of National Master Narratives in Southeast Asia', Journal of Contemporary Archival Studies, vol. 2, Article 4, 2015, p. 3.
51. Cristina Martinez-Juan, 'The Terms of War and Bontoc Eulogy: Studies in Re-Narrativizing Archival Forms', Southeast of Now: Directions in Contemporary and Modern Art in Asia, vol. 3, no. 2, 2019, p. 120, doi: 10.1353/sen.2019.0027.
52. See for example, Michelle Caswell and Marika Cifor, 'From Human Rights to Feminist Ethics: Radical Empathy in the Archives', Archivaria, vol. 81, Spring 2016, pp. 23–43; Cassie Findlay, 'Archival Activism', Archives and Manuscripts, vol. 44, no. 3, September 2016, pp. 155–9, doi: 10.1080/01576895.2016.1263964; Andrew Flinn, 'Archival Activism: Independent and Community-Led Archives, Radical Public History and the Heritage Professions', Interactions: UCLA Journal of Education and Information Studies, vol. 7, no. 2, 2011, pp. 1–20, doi: 10.5070/D472000699; Mark Greene, 'A Critique of Social Justice as an Archival Imperative: What Is It We're Doing That's All That Important?', The American Archivist, vol. 76, no. 2, September 2013, pp. 302–34, doi: 10.17723/aarc.76.2.14744l214663kw43; Makutla Mojapelo and Mpho Ngoepe, 'Advocacy as a Strategy to Raise the Archival Profile through the Civil Society in South Africa', Archives and Records, vol 43, no. 1, September 2020, pp. 18–35, doi: 10.1080/23257962.2020.1813095; James Roussain, 'Pedagogue in the Archive: Reorientating the Archivist as Educator', Archivaria, vol. 90, November 2020, pp. 70–111.
53. Terry Cook, p. 614, emphasis in original.
54. Two articles that provide useful background are Rodney G S Carter, 'Of Things Said and Unsaid: Power, Archival Silences, and Power in Silence', Archivaria, vol. 61, 2006, pp. 215–33; Verne Harris, 'Genres of the Trace: Memory, Archives and Trouble', Archives and Manuscripts, vol. 40, no. 3, November 2012, pp. 147–57, doi: 10.1080/01576895.2012.735825.

55. Yeo, p. 325.
56. Julia Kastenhofer, 'The Logic of Archival Authenticity: ISO 15489 and the Varieties of Forgeries in Archives', Archives and Manuscripts, vol. 43, no. 3, September 2015, p. 166, doi: 10.1080/01576895.2015.1074085.
57. Trace, p. 140.
58. Decker, p. 16.
59. See for example, Sarah Horton and Jacqueline Spence, 'Scoping the Economic and Social Impact of Archives', Undertaken for MLA Yorkshire. Aberystwyth: Department of Information Studies, University of Wales Aberystwyth, March 2006; Caitlin Patterson, 'Perceptions and Understandings of Archives in the Digital Age', The American Archivist, vol. 79, no. 2, September 2016, pp. 339–70, doi: 10.17723/0360-9081-79.2.339; Caroline Wavell, Graeme Baxter, Ian Johnson, and Dorothy Williams, 'Impact Evaluation of Museums, Archives and Libraries: Available Evidence Project', Aberdeen: Robert Gordon University, 2002, p. 70, available at https://www3.rgu.ac.uk/file/dorothy-williams-impact-evaluation-of-museums-archives-and-libraries-available-evidence-project, accessed 18 January 2023.
60. Cook, pp. 619–20.
61. Trace, p. 141.
62. Carbajal and Caswell, p. 1107.
63. Stephan, p. 5.
64. Trace, pp. 140–1.
65. See for example Bastian, 'Mine, Yours, Ours'; Karabinos, 'The Role of National Archives'.
66. See for example Green and Lee, p. 41.
67. Wavell, p. 41.
68. Bastian, p. 36.
69. Stephan, p. 2.
70. Cantillon, Baker, and Buttigieg, p. 10.
71. Greene, p. 304.
72. Caswell, Cole, and Griffith, p. 24.
73. Jimerson, p. 23.
74. Victoria Lemieux, 'Let the Ghosts Speak: An Empirical Exploration of the "Nature" of the Record', Archivaria, January 2001, pp. 81–111.
75. See for example, Ketelaar, 'Archivistics Research'; Eric Ketelaar, 'Tacit Narratives: The Meanings of Archives', Archival Science, vol. 1, no. 2, June 2001, pp. 131–41, doi: 10.1007/BF02435644; MacNeil, 2005; Mark A Matienzo and Dinah Handel, The Lighting the Way Handbook: Case Studies, Guidelines, and Emergent Futures for Archival Discovery and Delivery, Stanford University Libraries, Stanford, 2021; Elizabeth Yakel, 'Archival Representation', Archival Science, vol. 3, no. 1, March 2003, pp. 1–25, doi: 10.1007/BF02438926.
76. Cook, p. 600.
77. Green and Lee, p. 34.
78. See for example, Ciaran B Trace's discussion on the purpose versus the use of records, pp. 143–5.
79. See for example, Schwartz and Cook, 'Archives, Records, and Power'; Ciaran B Trace, 'What Is Recorded Is Never Simply "What Happened"'; Carbajal and Caswell, p. 1102, summarise this process well in relation to digital archives, stating 'how records came to be in digital archives, the infrastructures that maintain them, and the tools necessary to give access to and context for them – isn't ancillary to historical work but provides important context to do digital history better'.
80. Elizabeth Yakel and Deborah Torres, 'AI: Archival Intelligence and User Expertise', The American Archivist, vol. 66, no. 1, January 2003, p. 52, doi: 10.17723/aarc.66.1.q022h85pn51n5800.
81. Barros, Carneiro, and Wanderley, p. 288.
82. Decker, p. 15.
83. Lemieux, p. 94.
84. Cook, p. 606.
85. Ibid., p. 611.
86. See for example, Decker, 'The Silence of the Archives'; Carolina Fernandez-Quintanilla, 'Textual and Reader Factors in Narrative Empathy: An Empirical Reader Response Study Using Focus Groups', Language and Literature, vol. 29, no. 2, May 2020, pp. 124–46, doi: 10.1177/0963947020927134; Anne J Gilliland and Michelle Caswell, 'Records and Their Imaginaries: Imagining the Impossible, Making Possible the Imagined', Archival Science, vol. 16, no. 1, March 2016, pp. 53–75, doi: 10.1007/s10502-015-9259-z.
87. Horton and Spence, p. 44.

88. See for example, Carter.
89. Harris, p. 153.
90. Trace, p. 151.
91. Potter and Hepburn, p. 566.
92. Greene, p. 319.
93. See for example, Karin Speedy, 'Constructing Subaltern Silence in the Colonial Archive: An Australian Case Study', Journal of Australian Colonial History, vol. 18, 2016, pp. 95–114.
94. Bagnall and Sherratt, p. 284.
95. Lemieux, p. 93.
96. Carbajal and Caswell, p. 1107.
97. Yakel and Torres.
98. See for example, Carbajal and Caswell, 'Critical Digital Archives'; Charlton, 'The Treachery of Archives'; Colwell, 'Records Are Practices'; Paul Conway, 'Facts and Frameworks: An Approach to Studying the Users of Archives', The American Archivist, vol. 49, no. 4, October 1986, pp. 393–407, doi: 10.17723/aarc.49.4.p21825jp21403087; Karen Collins, 'Providing Subject Access to Images: A Study of User Queries', The American Archivist, vol. 61, no. 1, January 1998, pp. 36–55, doi: 10.17723/aarc.61.1.b531vt5q0q620642; Verne Harris, 'Genres of the Trace'; Pamela Mayer, 'Like a Box of Chocolates: A Case Study of User-Contributed Content at Footnote', The American Archivist, vol. 76, no. 1, April 2013, pp. 19–46, doi: 10.17723/aarc.76.1.up5u15p2k1826686; Kelvin L White and Anne J. Gilliland, 'Promoting Reflexivity and Inclusivity in Archival Education, Research, and Practice', The Library Quarterly: Information, Community, Policy, vol. 80, no. 3, July 2010, pp. 231–48, doi: 10.1086/652874.
99. An issue mentioned by (for example) Wendy M Duff and Catherine A Johnson, 'Accidentally Found on Purpose: Information-Seeking Behavior of Historians in Archives', The Library Quarterly, vol. 72, no. 4, October 2002, pp. 472–96, doi: 10.1086/lq.72.4.40039793; Hea Lim Rhee, 'Reflections on Archival User Studies', Reference & User Services Quarterly, vol. 54, no. 4, June 2015, pp. 29–42, doi: 10.5860/rusq.54n4.29; Polona Vilar and Alenka Šauperl, 'Archivists about Students as Archives Users', Information Research, vol. 22, no. 1, March 2017.
100. For example, Barros, Carneiro, and Wanderley, 'Organizational Archives and Historical Narratives'; Decker, 'The Silence of the Archives'.
101. Emily Ford, 'Tell Me Your Story: Narrative Inquiry in LIS Research', College & Research Libraries, vol. 81, no. 2, 2020, pp. 235–47, doi: 10.5860/crl.81.2.235; Celine Kearny, 'Narrative Inquiry: Writing Historiography', New Zealand Journal of Public History, vol. 5, no. 1, 2017, pp. 19–24.
102. Stephanie Decker, John Hassard, and Michael Rowlinson, 'Rethinking History and Memory in Organization Studies: The Case for Historiographical Reflexivity', Human Relations, vol. 74, no. 8, August 2021, pp. 1123–55, doi: 10.1177/0018726720927443.
103. Carolyn Ellis, Tony E Adams, and Arthur P Bochner, 'Autoethnography: An Overview', Forum Qualitative Sozialforschung / Forum: Qualitative Social Research, vol. 12, no. 1, 2011; Elysia Guzik, 'Representing Ourselves in Information Science Research: A Methodological Essay on Autoethnography / La Représentation de Nous-Mêmes Dans La Recherche En Sciences de l'information: Essai Méthodologique Sur l'auto-Ethnographie', Canadian Journal of Information and Library Science, vol. 37, no. 4, 2013, pp. 267–83, doi: 10.1353/ils.2013.0025.
104. Yakel and Torres, p. 51.
105. Stephan, p. 5.
106. See for example, Sanna Talja, 'Analyzing Qualitative Interview Data: The Discourse Analytic Method', Library and Information Science Research, vol. 21, no. 4, 1999, pp. 459–77, doi: 10.1016/S0740-8188(99)00024-9.
107. Audrey Alejandro, 'Reflexive Discourse Analysis: A Methodology for the Practice of Reflexivity', European Journal of International Relations, vol. 27, no. 1, 2021, pp. 150–74, doi: 10.1177/1354066120969789.
108. Eric Ketelaar and Viviane Frings-Hessami, 'Scholarly and Professional Communication in Archives: Archival Traditions and Languages', Archives & Manuscripts, vol. 49, no. 1–2, April 2021, pp. 1–7, doi: 10.1080/01576895.2021.1919043.
109. See for example, Green and Lee, 'From Transaction to Collaboration'; Michael Smith and Janet Villata, 'Applying User Centred Design to Archives', Archives & Manuscripts, vol. 48, no. 3, September 2020, pp. 239–49, doi: 10.1080/01576895.2020.1798790.
110. Marija Dalbello, 'Archaeological Sensations in the Archives of Migration and the Ellis Island Sensorium', Information Research, vol. 24, no. 2, June 2019, available at http://informationr.net/ir/24-2/paper817.html, accessed 18 January 2023.
111. Cook, p. 613.

REFLECTION ARTICLE

Hunters and Collectors: The Work of ABC's News Libraries Across Archives and TV News Production

Benjamin Pask

Australian Broadcasting Corporation, Sydney, NSW, Australia

Abstract

This reflection aims to acknowledge and celebrate the work of the Australian Broadcasting Corporation's TV News Libraries in the wake of their closure in December 2022 as part of an ABC Archives restructure.

Keywords: *Television; News; Australian Broadcasting Corporation*

Television news libraries have two primary functions: to archive news/current affairs content and to supply audiovisual material for reporters to tell their stories. Working across the disparate sectors of archives and news production, the scope of their work may not be fully appreciated by either. With ABC closing its TV News Libraries in December 2022, I wish to acknowledge their achievements by presenting an overview of their duties and to reflect upon my time as a News Library Cataloguer and Researcher based in ABC's Ultimo Centre in Sydney. This is a reflection on my singular experiences in the role, and does not seek to represent the corporation nor my former colleagues.

The archival work undertaken by News Libraries focused around collecting three strands of audiovisual material: off-air recordings of news/current affairs broadcasts, 'edit master' versions of news/current affairs stories, and the raw material generated in the process of newsgathering.

Unlike off-air recordings, edit master versions of stories are 'clean' copies without 'supers' (i.e., on-screen text identifying personalities, locations, etc.). Audio elements may be split across separate channels, making it possible for editors reusing parts of these stories to mute a reporter or contributor's voice while retaining natural background sound. These features make edit masters a useful production asset, and they were catalogued with considerable detail.

The expansion of news/current affairs into online media presented a challenge to News Libraries, with stories frequently published in several iterations across multiple platforms and bulletins. This required libraries to identify and retain the optimal version of a story, which may be the longest version, or that with the most unique ABC-owned material.

---

*Correspondence: Benjamin Pask, Email: benpask@gmail.com

News Libraries also selected raw camera material to retain as library assets, a process that involved removing superfluous content (e.g., 'colour bar' test patterns), adding metadata, applying standardized naming and archiving to protected folders. When I joined the ABC in 2009, TV News was transitioning to tapeless production and the Library was selecting material from a handful of camera tapes and files every day. The volume of material passing through ABC newsrooms expanded massively over the past decade, and at my time of departure in December 2022, we were selecting from over 200 items daily in Sydney alone. This included not only footage shot by ABC's outstanding news crews in Australia and across the world, but those of other newsgathering services – public service and commercial – who share footage as part of news pool agreements. This 'pool footage' can often be retained, reused and sold in the same way as that originating from ABC crews and forms a sizable part of this collection.

News Libraries were attached to ABC newsrooms in state and territory capitals across Australia. Each library collected material unique to their location, with librarians bringing local knowledge to their selection and cataloguing of raw media. Special mention must be made of Canberra's News Library, whose exhaustive collection of Australian federal politics complements the work carried out by the Parliamentary Library. Each state and territory library's collection can be accessed by their counterparts across the country.

ABC News Libraries' collection of raw media neatly illustrates the critical importance of professionally applied metadata. Consider, for instance, the news pool helicopter that takes off from Sydney every day to gather an hour or two of footage through the bubble-mounted camera on its undercarriage. Its meandering journey tends to be dominated by the waterways over which aviation law dictates the chopper must, where possible, fly. There is limited value in retaining this daily flight in its unexamined raw state but identifying, isolating and adding relevant metadata to any news events recorded (e.g., a flood in a specific location, a road accident or a crime scene), as well as any notable footage captured along the way (e.g., a wedge-tailed eagle soaring on the updraft of a bushfire, a new suburb springing up along the urban fringe, a Royal Australian Navy (RAN) warship sailing to dock at Garden Island) can convert this rough material into a valued resource. Experienced News Librarians took their knowledge of the existing collection to the practice of selection, seeking to retain material that updated and expanded the archive, maximizing the value of footage shot by newsgathering crews, and broadening the resources at hand when responding to journalists' requests for footage.

This collection may be the News Libraries' greatest legacy. It is not only a valuable production asset, but a national treasure offering an unfiltered window into Australian life, from bushfires and pandemics to leadership spills and mullet festivals. It is an order of magnitude more objective than broadcast news, largely avoiding accusations of bias directed at edited storytelling. There are, of course, factors influencing what a camera operator records and what a News Library opts to retain, but there is an undeniable streak of veracity running through this collection.

The Libraries' professional selection practices and application of metadata transformed this raw media into a legacy of hundreds of thousands of archival assets. This is not some rarely opened vault representing bygone times, but a living collection in constant expansion and daily use. You can see some of it this evening, on the *7pm News*.

Library footage is a major and essential component of television news and current affairs, and ABC News Library researchers worked rostered shifts across mornings, evenings and weekends to support different bulletins and supply this footage to content makers. Library footage is present in most news/current affairs stories. It is the crime scene shown in a report on a court case; it is the accused walking outside court and the aerial shot of a prison used in a later report on their sentencing. It constitutes the majority of many types of story: obituaries, political retirements, 'backgrounders' on historical or current events, or profiles of public figures.

Research requests for library footage came from journalists, editors or producers and were immensely variable in scope, scale and subject. A politics reporter may ask for a specific quote ('… can I have Tony Burke's presser from 1 November 2022, when he says…') or a non-specific quote ('… can I have a cabinet minister saying *something like*…') and so a working knowledge of Hansard and awareness of speech transcript resources was useful. Reporters may request a specific location ('… can I have federal parliament exteriors…') or a specific location with a qualitative modifier ('… can I have a *guilty building* shot of federal parliament…'). A 'guilty building' describes a low-angle shot in crepuscular conditions, possibly with some unidentifiable silhouetted ne'er-do-wells in the frame. 'Guilty building' shots of federal parliament, it will surprise no-one to learn, are of greater value to a News Library than a 'hopeful' shot of the building bathed in a glorious rose-tinted sunrise.

Despite the breadth of ABC's own archives, it was often necessary to search for footage outside the corporation. ABC has usage agreements with several international press agencies, while C-SPAN and the White House's YouTube channel became increasingly useful as coverage of USA politics ballooned over recent years. State and federal parliamentary libraries were an outstanding resource, while user-generated content (UGC) also had its place, particularly in events such as natural disasters where smartphone-wielding first responders and local residents recorded dramatic pictures ahead of news crews.

News Librarians had to be cognisant of any rights or restrictions related to footage sought by content-makers, holding third-party (i.e., non-ABC) material up to particular scrutiny. Footage germane to a story may be permissible under Fair Dealing for reporting of News,[1] but this is by no means a universal get-out clause allowing kleptomaniacal footage-grabbing. ABC newsrooms have access to a legal team with rights expertise, but outside of core business hours such advice was often provided by News Library researchers.

Third-party material frequently brought technical difficulties alongside rights issues. ABC News Library researchers became adept at the messy business of downloading embedded online videos and wrangling these troublesome files into news production systems. News Librarians demonstrated expertise across these systems, troubleshooting technical issues and facilitating file transfers between ABC sites.

'Overlay' became an increasingly common term in research requests after the launch of ABC's 24-hour news channel in 2010. 'Overlay' describes establishing footage of a news event, location or personality that will *overlay* (i.e., be screened over) a reporter, presenter or interview subject's voice. Preferred overlay of a personality shows them walking, working at a desk or close-mouthed in a cutaway from a press conference. Close-mouthed because, if they are shown talking, it can lead to the dissonant 'goldfishing' effect where the voiceover appears to originate from the subject's lips.

With its busy roster of guests and experts, ABC's news channel had a constant hunger for overlay, with some typical requests as follows:

'We've got the amphibian keeper from Taronga Zoo on the 11am bulletin. We're gonna need some overlay of Australia's threatened frog species'. This is a straightforward one – find the frogs.

'There's a population expert coming on. Can we please get overlay of, um, people doing… stuff, I guess?' A vague request like this can be deceptively tricky. ABC News endeavours to represent Australia in all its diversity, and the researcher must reflect this in their choices.

Mark Seymour from Hunters & Collectors is coming onto The Drum *this evening to talk about the state of live music in Australian cities. Can we please get some of their video clips, maybe some live performances, and some recent pics of newer bands playing smaller venues?*

Time to dive into the *Rage* database for those music videos, as well as searching for any performances on programs such as *Countdown* while checking for any library footage showing the live music scene around Australia.

'*Our guest at Midday will be discussing Australia Day. Can we please get some celebrations, maybe some barbecues,* Hottest 100 *parties, some Invasion Day protests, and some shots of the First Fleet arriving?*' Yes, yes, yes, yes and… a News Library researcher should try to avoid saying 'no'. We could, then, explain that the First Fleet arrived a century or so before the moving image while offering some footage of historical drawings and watercolours depicting the colonists' landing.

Television news is unpredictable. Research will be busy, and it will be last minute. ABC's Ultimo Centre in Sydney houses a videotape vault two floors above the News Library's former location. Sometimes, when a story breaks with minutes to the bulletin, that archival vault airlock takes twice as long as usual to open and those compactus handles cannot spin fast enough before the researcher runs, tape in hand and gasping for breath, to ingest that much-needed library footage into the news system with seconds to spare and an impatient phone ringing. Television newsrooms can crackle with energy, and there were many occasions when the News Library phone was lifted to hear a voice shaking with adrenaline.

Perhaps the *Archives and Manuscripts* reader shudders at this. I know that I did. When setting out on a career in archives I had an image of myself alone with a Steenbeck[2] and stack of film cans in a dimly lit room, engrossed in contemplative, detail-oriented work. I dreaded scenarios like that of the previous paragraph and was hesitant to take a position in the News Library. It could be high-adrenaline, high-stakes work. I did not want to 'break the news' (in the sense of somehow preventing it from going to air).

And so I was astonished to find myself loving it. I loved hearing that adrenalized voice on the other end of the phone melt with relief as we got the library footage to make their story. I loved seeing our work on ABC's flagship news and current affairs programs moments after we had provided it. I loved being part of the stories that defined our nation – gathering around a newsroom monitor as a prime minister is usurped, helping an editor find the perfect shot to bring a lead story to life, or smelling bushfire smoke as I passed a reporter's desk – but most of all I loved working with my fellow News Librarians. This team of great experience and diverse expertise was supportive, collaborative and indefatigable in their commitment to finding the best possible footage to tell a news story.

At least twenty archive professionals lost ABC News Library positions at the end of 2022, with management pushing a self-service research model onto newsrooms, and much of their archival work shifted to automated processes. I wish my few remaining colleagues the best in the challenging circumstances of their continuing employment, and hope that these cuts do not precipitate the decline in journalistic and archival standards anticipated by ALIA, the ASA,[3] and many other individuals and professional organisations.

Notes

1. Australian Copyright Council, Information Sheet G079v09, p. 4, available at https://www.copyright.org.au/browse/book/ACC-Fair-Dealing:-What-Can-I-Use-Without-Permission-INFO079, accessed 18 January 2023.
2. Steenbeck is a brand of film editor machine favoured by film archives for viewing 16 mm and 35 mm film material, available at https://en.wikipedia.org/wiki/Steenbeck, accessed 18 January 2023.
3. Australian Library and Information Association: Open letter on proposed cuts to ABC library and archive professional roles, available at https://www.alia.org.au/Web/News/Articles/2022/June-2022/Open-letter-on-proposed-cuts-to-ABC.aspx, accessed 19 January 2023.

Archives & Manuscripts

REFLECTION ARTICLE

Archiving Visual Effects: Filling a Digital Void in the Documented Memory of Film and Television

Evanthia Samaras

University of Technology Sydney

Abstract

Digital visual effects emerged onto cinema screens during the mid-20th century and have now become an essential feature of contemporary film and television production. Notwithstanding the rise and prominence of visual effects in the telecinematic discourse as a key visual storytelling tool, there is currently a visual effects gap in audiovisual archival collections, and a digital void in the documented memory of film and television. Why are there no visual effects records in our moving image archives?

This reflection will explore the above question by sharing some findings from my doctoral research about records and archiving in the global film and television visual effects industry.

Keywords: *Archives; Film; Special effects; Television; Visual effects.*

Introduction

Before entering the archive profession in 2013, I muddled my way through various media advertising and production jobs following the completion of a media production undergraduate degree. Despite my failings to establish a genuine career in the media industry, my affinity for screen production did not waver. So, when a new screen animation and visual effects school opened at the University of Technology Sydney, I jumped at the opportunity to join its research cohort to undertake a PhD about visual effects records and archiving.

For almost 4 years, I embarked on an inclusive doctoral research study with the film and television visual effects industry to document its unique recordkeeping landscape. My goal was to determine how improvements (which align to archival theory and methods and established cultural heritage collection practices) could be effectively adopted in the industry, to support the ongoing business of visual effects production and to encourage the formation of archive collections. As part of the research, I investigated the collections of 10 major international film and television archives to determine if they were collecting visual effects material. I was surprised to discover that visual effects records are barely seen in any of their collections. How could this be?

While visual effects copyright plays a sizeable role, my research uncovered other reasons, all of which I will present in this reflection, to illuminate and hopefully explain why – despite

*Correspondence: Evanthia Samaras Email: evanthia.samaras@alumni.uts.edu.au

having existed as part of mainstream film and television production for decades – visual effects records have not been duly archived to date.

Before embarking further into this reflection, some terminology requires addressing. Visual effects and special effects are terms used in the context of film and television production to denote 'artificially contrived effects designed to create the illusion of real (or imagined) events'.[1] In contemporary industry vernacular, 'visual effects' or 'VFX' are the processes through which imagery is *digitally* altered, created, or enhanced, while 'special effects' or 'SFX' are practical effects that are *physically* implemented directly on set and captured during the live-action shoot. Given contemporary visual effects work is inherently a digital creative and technical process, predictably, records of the visual effects industry are predominately created and managed in digital formats.

Now that the lingo has been established, I will now provide a very brief history of visual effects to provide important context and illustrate its long-standing place within telecinematic discourse,[2] history, and culture.

A brief overview of visual effects

The very first example of digital effects in a film is the opening credits of Alfred Hitchcock's 1958 film Vertigo. Tom Sito describes the computer animation sequence as 'complicated graphics that spiral out from still photos of actress Kim Novak's eyes, all set to the eerie music of Bernard Hermann'.[3] The designer of the sequence, Saul Bass, insisted that the spirals be accurate and not be drawn freehand. John Whitney was hired to help Bass bring his design into fruition by developing an animation rig using a World War II, 850-lbs anti-aircraft targeting computer.[4]

Following this innovation, many others soon followed from Whitney and other digital pioneers such as Douglas Trumball and John Dykstra; until digital technologies started to become more standardized, and audiences began to grow accustomed to digital visual effects through the success of science fiction films such as 2001: A Space Odyssey (1968), Westworld (1973), and Star Wars (1977).[5]

As Shilo McClean indicates, it was during the 1980s that the use of digital visual effects began to really take off, through accelerated advancements in computer software and hardware.[6] Then, in the 1990s, as the technologies became more affordable, the digital spectacles accelerated and translated to lucrative box office success through titles, such as Terminator 2: Judgement Day (1991) and Jurassic Park (1993), as well as Toy Story (1995), which was the first feature film produced entirely from computer animation technology.[7,8]

While practical special effects are still adopted, in the 21st century, visual effects are now a commonplace and necessary feature of film and television. As the Executive Creative of Zoic Studios says, 'Creative crossover between feature film and television is reaching its peak, [...] upp[ing] the game in creative visual problem-solving for VFX [...]'.[9]

Overall, the visual effects industry holds both financial and cultural importance in Australasia and other regions of the world. On average, 20–25% of production budgets are spent on visual effects.[10] In 2019, the global visual effects services market worth was $3.9 billion USD and is forecasted to reach $8.9 billion by the end of 2026.[11] The industry employs thousands of digital artists to generate imagery for wide-reaching media content for big and small screens. Using an array of ever-developing digital technologies, commercial software, and bespoke tools and code; visual effects practitioners craft and combine 3D models, animations, environments, and lighting elements output as 'shots'[12] for film and television productions.

Searching for digital visual effects records in moving image collections

For my research, I searched for visual effects records in the following libraries, archives, and museums (LAMs), selected for their extensive experience in collecting moving image records, and their availability of resources in the English language (see Table 1).

Table 1. Libraries, archives, and museums investigated

Name	Country
Academy of Motion Picture Arts and Sciences' Film Archive, Museum and the Margaret Herrick Library	United States of America
Australian Centre for the Moving Image (ACMI)	Australia
British Film Institute (BFI)	United Kingdom
Deutsche Kinemathek	Germany
Eye Film Museum	Netherlands
Institut national de l'audiovisuel (INA)	France
Lucas Museum of Narrative Art	United States of America
National Film and Sound Archive of Australia (NFSA)	Australia
University of California Los Angeles (UCLA) Film and TV Archive and Library	United States of America
University of Southern California (USC) School of Cinematic Arts collections including Hugh M. Hefner Moving Image Archive	United States of America

When my searches across catalogs and available literature proved inconclusive, I emailed collection specialists from the LAMs to obtain definitive information about whether they had digital visual effects records in their collections.

Through the investigation, I found that the LAMs appear to have a proclivity to acquire *material* film and television effects-related records and artifacts (this even applies to records about digital visual effects). Examples include production photographs of models and sets[13]; film still prints featuring visual effects[14]; correspondence, scripts, illustrations, and budgets concerning special effects[15,16]; breakdown documents about scenes requiring special effects[17]; original hand-drawn sketches for various matte shots[18]; camera and projection devices and equipment such as Dave Drzewiecki's horizontal VistaVision projectors and 35 mm film clips used on various film effects shots.[19]

The limited examples of digital visual effects records I could identify included a showreel from VFX company Animal Logic in Media Exchange Format (.mxf) and MPEG-4 (.mp4) formats at NFSA,[20] and VFX image sequences in Digital Picture Exchange (.dpx) format from two film projects in the Eye Film Museum collection.[21]

In addition, records from a single film or television title tended to be dispersed between studio archives, university and public LAMs, and private collections. For example, when searching for relevant Star Trek records, I had no luck in finding any digital visual effects records. However, I did find that the hand-crafted U.S.S. Enterprise Model from the original Star Trek television series is held in the Smithsonian's National Air and Space Museum collection.[22] A photo mechanical print of the Enterprise model is located at the Academy's Margaret Herrick Library.[23] An original matte painting from the series can be found at the commercial Science Fiction Archives in Hollywood,[24] and numerous other matte paintings from the various iterations of the television series have been sold to private collectors at auction. Furthermore, the UCLA Library has a unique collection of hardcopy production papers from Dan Curry, the Visual Effects Producer of Star Trek: The Next Generation, Star Trek: Deep Space Nine, Star Trek: Voyager, and Star Trek: Enterprise.[25] With all these Star Trek records being geographically dispersed among multiple collecting institutions, provenance and original order are considerably compromised.

Why are contemporary, digital visual effects records missing from LAM collections? The following section of the reflection will explore this question by presenting 4 reasons.

Reason 1. Copyright and intellectual property

Copyright legislation in both Australia and the USA indicates that the producer of a film or television project (generally a studio, network, or streaming platform) is the 'owner' of the project's visual effects work. The work of visual companies and their staff is considered 'work made for hire'.[26] In the Unites States, work made for hire projects has a copyright period of 120 years after creation or 95 years after publication, whichever is shorter.[27]

Because the studios, networks, and streaming platforms are the 'owners' of film and television visual effects work, the visual effects records are considered their intellectual property. Hence, it is not in their economic interest to make their records available freely to archives. For example, Disney Marvel employs Digital Asset Coordinators to help the studio collate and organize their 'asset'[28] records and associated metadata in their Marvel Asset Library.[29] Collecting the asset records protects their intellectual property and helps facilitate their reuse on multiple films. As a visual effects practitioner explained to me:

> Anything that is a franchise [the studios] will care [about], so on Deadpool they really want their stuff, they want all the effects for X-Men. Whereas something like True Grit [the studio will] not ask for their snake. Because they don't care.[30]

However, given the fast rate of technology obsolescence, digital files are unlikely to be readable and usable after a decade. So, their value to the studios, networks, and streaming platforms will quickly diminish. If placed in custody of an archive with established digital preservation programs, digital visual effects records are more likely to be managed, preserved, and accessible over time, than if they remain under their owner's control. This approach is also supported by the fact that there is already an established precedent for film and television records to be donated to publicly accessible LAMs. For instance, the University of Southern California has a huge collection of Warner Bros. paper records in their collection.[31]

Arguably, copyright and intellectual property are major factors contributing to the lack of available visual effects collections. However, there are other reasons, which I uncovered during my research.

Reason 2. Acquisition policies: The missing backbone

As the Canadian Council of Archives describes, a collection policy, or acquisition policy, is:

> [An] instrument which provides the archival institution with the direction for making appraisal and acquisition decisions and allocating resources. It is the backbone around which the archival institution can acquire comprehensive holdings in a planned, coordinated, and systematic manner.[32]

Without this 'backbone', it would be difficult for visual effects records to be identified and transferred into collections. Hence, as part of my research I examined, if 'visual effects' were mentioned in the acquisition policies of my selected 10 moving image LAMs. I located policies for 8 of the 10 LAMs, and only one – the Academy of Motion Picture Arts and Sciences, included a section on screen effects records: 'Special effects demonstration reels and elements' that were submitted as part of the Academy's Scientific and Technical Awards.[33] Disappointingly, these records solely relate to the development of visual effects software and tools. Visual effects records created for specific film and television production projects are completely missing from the policy.

Interestingly, policies from ACMI, BFI, EYE Filmmuseum, and NFSA do include remits to collect video games and/or immersive media (virtual, augmented, and mixed reality) – works encompassing digital records that have the same, or similar qualities and technical requirements to film and television visual effects records.

In addition to copyright legislation and acquisition policies, the remaining two notions presented in this reflection diverge into the intangible realms of human psychology and culture.

Reason 3. Material records foster engagement and the numinous experience

Another reason to explain the lack of digital visual effects records in collections is that they do not foster engagement and the numinous experience, like material records do.

Emmanuel Tsekleves suggests that the 'physical is deeply imprinted in our biological and psychological makeup'; hence, even though we live in a digital world, the appeal of analogue is more akin to who we are and 'how we make sense of our world'.[34] In a study comparing user experiences with physical archival records and their digital surrogates, Anastasia Varnalis-Weigle found that material records tended to provide more engagement and provoked a stronger emotional response in accordance with the complexity and level of interest in the record.[35] It was also discovered that a numinous affect was only experienced with a physical object.[36]

Maines and Glynn describe the numinosity of an artifact as having a real or imagined association with a person, place, or event bestowed with 'special sociocultural magic' and which 'carries emotional weight with the viewer'.[37] The numinous experience is transformative and mysterious, and the personal connection forged with an object not only manifests admiration and wonderment but can also produce 'deep engagement, empathy or spiritual communion'.[38] For example, in a study about the numinosity of museum objects, Kiersten Latham noticed that all the participants were 'deeply touched by the experience, describing connections that transcended memory, time, and self'.[39]

Furthermore, interviews with VFX practitioners, which I conducted as part of my research, also revealed that they too have an affinity for physical records:

> Visual effects people tend to hold in very high regard the people that do, special effects – practical special effects. Which is why, we love having like swords [or] prop[s] [from] film[s] that we worked on [...] We love having these things around, that tangible aspect to it.[40]

The material record no doubt has some qualities that its immaterial, digital counterparts do not possess. What does this mean for an entire field of film and television production practice that predominately generates digital records? Will records of the visual effects industry ever appeal to LAM audiences? Perhaps more time needs to pass, so that there is more of a historical quality to the visual records. Yet, the longer we wait, the more likely the records will become unreadable and inaccessible due to technology progression and lack of available legacy tools and software.

Reason 4. VFX gets a bad rap (or is rendered invisible)

The final reason I would like to present to explain why digital visual effects records are missing from collections, relates to longstanding negative generalizations and erasure afforded to visual effects work.

As Sonya Teich notes, in the moment when Star Wars (1977) was awarded Best Visual Effects at the Academy Awards, it was also 'being pointed to as the destroyer of the auteur renaissance'.[41] Then, as digital visual effects flourished in the 1990s in films such as Jurassic Park (1993), they were considered by some as dwelling on 'visual spectacle for its own sake'.[42] Visual effects during this time were described as 'a hallucinatory excess'[43], 'an eclipse to narrative, plot and character'[44], and 'the antithesis of narrative'.[45]

These negative generalizations have continued to present day. For example, when describing Avengers: Age of Ultron (2015), Variety critic Brian Lowry indicates that the computer-generated imagery 'wizardry' has 'become a curse', and 'while the results can be visually astounding, the movies regularly feel as lifeless and mechanized as the technology responsible for bringing those visions to fruition'.[46]

Moreover, even film directors speak of them negatively:

While [JJ] Abrams touted 2015's Star Wars: The Force Awakens as a return to the practical aesthetic of the original trilogy, roughly 2,100 shots in the film used VFX. In reference to 2017's Dunkirk, [Christopher] Nolan said: 'The older techniques are working better. With visual effects, after a while the contemporary tricks look cheaper'.[47]

While visual effects have received negative critique, at the same time, it is often erased or unacknowledged – it is a hidden job.[48] With regard to media coverage of visual effects work, Mihaela Mihailova highlights:

Crucial information, such as the nature, extent, and relative importance of animators and visual effects artists' specific contributions is typically glossed over or completely omitted (except in specialized trade publications such as Cinefex and VFX World Magazine).[49]

Similarly, the extent of visual effects motion capture work required to bring computer-generated characters to life can be brushed off. Actor and director Andy Serkis, known for his work as the Gollum character in the Lord of the Rings films and Caesar in the Planet of the Apes movies, has stated that 'the authorship of performance – everything you watch on screen that you feel and think about a character – comes from the actor'.[50] This act of claiming responsibility for the entire performance does not acknowledge that motion capture work is actually a collaboration between the actor and numerous visual effects artists.[51]

Overall, these generalizations and erasure of VFX labor spouted by film critics and practitioners have unfortunately entered the collective societal psyche, affecting the comprehension and appreciation of visual effects work.

Visual effects are worthy of collecting

In this reflection, I have presented four reasons, uncovered during my doctoral research to explore why visual effects records have not been duly archived to date.

It is my hope that archivists, librarians, and curators will begin the journey toward addressing the visual effects gap in our film and television cultural heritage collections and realize that visual effects records are worthy of collecting. I encourage readers in these positions to make connections with studios, networks, streaming platforms, and visual effects companies to explore ways to document the memory of visual effects and collect and share visual effects records. So, the history and legacy of this significant half-century canon of our digital screen history and culture will not be lost and forgotten.

Acknowledgments

I would like to thank Professors Andrew Johnston and Elise van den Hoven from the University of Technology Sydney, for their supervision and mentorship throughout the research.

Notes

1. Steve Blandford, The film studies dictionary, Arnold, London, 2000.
2. Telecinematic discourse is the language of film and television, the audio and visual elements that communicate, represent, and convey meaning to audiences through narrative and production techniques. See Roberta Piazza, Monika Bednarek, and Fabio Rossi, Telecinematic discourse: approaches to the language of films and television series, John Benjamins, Philadelphia, PA, 2011.
3. Tom Sito, Moving innovation: a history of computer animation, MIT Press, Cambridge, MA, 2013, p. 28.
4. Computer Animation History, Vertigo (1957), 2018, available at https://computeranimationhistory-cgi.jimdofree.com/vertigo/, accessed 17 September 2022.
5. Rama Venkatasawmy, The digitization of cinematic visual effects: Hollywood's coming of age, Lexington Books, Blue Ridge Summit, PA, 2012, pp. 48–56.
6. Shilo T. McClean, Digital storytelling: the narrative power of visual effects in film, MIT Press, Cambridge, MA, 2014.
7. Mark Henne, Hal Hickel, Ewan Johnson, and Sonoks Konishi, 'The making of Toy Story', in Proceedings of the 41st IEEE Computer Society International Conference: Technologies for the Information Superhighway, IEEE Computer Society Press, Los Alamitos, CA, 25–28 February 1996, pp. 463–8.
8. McClean.
9. Andrew Orloff, 'The future of VFX for television', Post, vol. 32, no. 1, 2017, p. 33.
10. Research and Markets, 'Global animation, VFX & video games industry: strategies, trends & opportunities, (2020–25)', 2020, available at https://www.researchandmarkets.com/reports/4900485/global-animation-vfx-and-video-games-industry, accessed 17 September 2022.
11. 360 Market Updates, 'Global visual effects services market size, status and forecast 2020–2026', 2020, available at https://www.360marketupdates.com/global-visual-effects-services-market-14858457, accessed 17 September 2022.
12. A shot, also known as a take, is an uninterrupted series of frames, which could last from several seconds to several minutes.
13. Margaret Herrick Library, 1089A Arnold Gillespie photographs (1936–1962).
14. Margaret Herrick Library, 70010263-4 Film stills featuring visual effects from War of the Worlds (2005).
15. Margaret Herrick Library, 426 Linwood G. Dunn papers (1902–2001).
16. UCLA Library Special Collections, LSC.2294 Dan Curry papers (1967–2008).
17. British Film Institute, Series JCL-12 Something Wicked This Way Comes (c1976–1985).
18. British Film Institute, Series BED122 Design production files for Black Narcissus (1946).
19. Personal correspondence, USC School of Cinematic Arts, 1 June 2019.
20. National Film and Sound Archive of Australia, 751368 Animal Logic Showreel (1996).
21. Eye Film Museum, KOP1230907 Jackie trailer working material (2012) and KOP1233229 Snackbar working material (2012).
22. Smithsonian National Air and Space Museum, A19740668000 Star Trek Starship Enterprise studio model (1966).
23. Margaret Herrick Library, 70121493 Photomechanical print of the U.S.S. Enterprise, Star Trek (c1967).
24. Science Fiction Archives, 589 Original starbase 11 matte painting from Star Trek: The Original Series.
25. UCLA Library Special Collections, LSC.2294 Dan Curry papers (1967–2008).
26. Copyright Act of 1976 (USA), §101.
27. Copyright Act of 1976 (USA), §302.
28. Asset is a term used in visual effects to describe a digitally crafted 3D or 2D object and its parts. For example, a 3D asset may include model, texture and rig assets.
29. Marvel Entertainment, 'Digital asset coordinator', LinkedIn, available at https://www.linkedin.com/jobs/view/digital-asset-coordinator-at-marvel-entertainment-395831884, accessed 17 September 2022.
30. Senior VFX Producer, 1 March 2019.
31. See University of Southern California School of Cinematic Arts, 'Warner Bros. Archives', 2016, available at https://cinema.usc.edu/about/warnerbrosarchives.cfm, accessed 17 September 2022.
32. Canadian Council of Archives. Guidelines for Developing an Acquisition Policy, Archives Association of British Columbia, Ontario, March 1990, available at https://web.archive.org/web/20160627101739; https://aabc.ca/STORAGE/Toolkit_storage/Toolkit_files_old_linked/toolkit_guidelines_for_an_acquisition_policy.html, accessed 17 September 2022.
33. Academy of Motion Picture Arts and Sciences, 'About the archive', 2018, available at https://www.oscars.org/academy-film-archive/about-archive, accessed 17 September 2022.

34. Emmanuel Tsekleves, 'The enduring appeal of analogue in a digital world', The Conversation, 2015, available at https://theconversation.com/the-enduring-appeal-of-analogue-in-a-digital-world-35790, accessed 17 September 2022.
35. Varnalis-Weigle, Anastasia S. (2016) 'A Comparative Study of User Experience between Physical Objects and Their Digital Surrogates,' Journal of Contemporary Archival Studies: Vol. 3, Article 3. Available at: http://elischolar.library.yale.edu/jcas/vol3/iss1/3
36. ibid.
37. Rachel P Maines and James J Glynn, 'Numinous objects', The Public Historian, vol. 15, no. 1, 1993, pp. 9–25.
38. Catherine M Cameron and John B Gatewood, 'Seeking numinous experiences in the unremembered past', Ethnology, vol. 42, no. 1, 2003, pp. 55–71.
39. Kiersten F Latham, 'Numinous experiences with museum objects', Visitor Studies, vol. 16, no. 1, 2013, pp. 3–20.
40. Senior VFX Pipeline Specialist, 15 July 2019.
41. Sonya Teich, 'Auteur vs computer: the frightening complexity of visual effects', The Conversation, 6 July 2020, available at https://theconversation.com/auteur-vs-computer-the-frightening-complexity-of-visual-effects-131458, accessed 17 September 2022.
42. Stephen Prince, 'Through the looking glass: philosophical toys and digital visual effects', Projections: The Journal for Movies and Mind, vol. 4, no. 2, 2010, pp. 19–40.
43. Scott Bukatman, Matters of gravity: special effects and supermen in the 20th century, Duke University Press, Durham, NC, 2003, p. 113.
44. Annette Kuhn, Alien zone II: the spaces of science-fiction cinema, Verso, London, 1999, p. 5.
45. Andrew Darley, Visual digital culture: surface play and spectacle in new media genres, Routledge, London, 2000, p. 104.
46. Brian Lowry, 'Avengers' and the age of CGI overkill in Hollywood', Variety, 4 May 2015, available at https://variety.com/2015/film/news/avengers-age-of-ultron-cgi-special-effects-1201487125, accessed 17 September 2022.
47. Teich 2020.
48. Teich 2020.
49. Mihaela Mihailova, 'Collaboration without representation: labor issues in motion and performance capture', Animation, vol. 11, no. 1, 2016, pp. 40–58.
50. John Hiscock, 'Andy Serkis interview: "audiences are moved by acting, not effects"', The Telegraph, 10 July 2014, available at https://www.telegraph.co.uk/culture/film/film-news/10956372/Andy-Serkis-interview-Audiences-are-moved-by-acting-not-effects.html, accessed 17 September 2022.
51. Ceren Balci, 'Technological construction of performance: case of Andy Serkis', MA thesis, İhsan Doğramacı Bilkent University, 2016.

REFLECTION ARTICLE

The *Music and the First World War* Project at the Australian War Memorial

Theresa Cronk

Star of the Sea College and Westbourne Grammar School, Melbourne

Abstract

The *Music and the First World War* project was a First World War centenary project at the Australian War Memorial that involved the digitisation of a selection of diaries, letters, concert programs and 100 pieces of sheet music held in the Memorial's collection. This article examines the process of developing the project, preparing the collections for digitisation and establishing a publishing framework for online release. The article also discusses some of the benefits of the project for telling the stories of each of these songs, their history and the performers involved.

Keywords: *Digitisation; First World War; Music; Collection management databases; Arrangement and Description*

This article focuses on the *Music and the First World War* project at the Australian War Memorial and is based on a conference paper that was delivered at the Australian Society of Archivists annual conference in 2021. The paper, and this article, outlined the development of the *Music and the First World War* project, preparation of the supporting collections for digitisation, and the establishment of a publishing framework to deliver the original project concept. The benefits of the project for telling the stories of each of the selected songs, their history and the performers involved will also be described. Also, incorporated into this article are some of the stories about the songs and the performers that were uncovered as part of the project.

The *Music and the First World War* project was based at the Research Centre of the Australian War Memorial ('the Memorial'). The Research Centre collections include the Memorial's official records; library collections, including sheet music; and personal diaries and letters.

The *Music and the First World War* project brought together the collections of diaries and letters that contained strong musical references, concert programs and sheet music (Figures 1 and 2). It also commissioned modern recordings of 100 pieces of sheet music held in the Memorial's collection. At the heart of this project was the digitisation of these collections and displaying this material online in a meaningful way that allowed researchers to view the historical context of the performances and literature around a selection of 100 songs. The intention of the project was

---

*Correspondence: Theresa Cronk, Email: theresa_cronk@hotmail.com

Figure 1. Excerpt from sheet music for 'Somewhere a voice is calling me'.[2]

Figure 2. Except from cover of sheet music for 'Give me dear Australia'.[3]

to make music of the First World War period more accessible to a wider audience. All elements of the *Music and the First World War* project were brought together as an online exhibition. The online exhibition deliverable can be accessed via the Memorial's website.[1]

Work on the *Music and the First World War* project commenced in 2014. The project evolved out of research being undertaken at the time into the Research Centre collection to find stories relevant to music during the First World War period. There was interest in doing something with this research so that the knowledge could be shared and not disappear back into the archives. From the beginning, this was a very ambitious project that contained several outputs. In early 2017, the overall project was divided into four phases. At that time, it was estimated that the project would take another 2 years to complete.

The first phase of this project involved identifying diaries and letters in the Research Centre collection that mentioned titles of songs, references to musical performances or a strong connection with a musical performer or bandsman as well as printed sheet music or concert programs. A subject-based collection guide for sheet music held in the collection, related to the First World War, was also to be published online during this part of the project.

The second phase involved the online release of sound recordings specifically recorded for this project and the digitised version of associated collection items (diaries, letters, published sheet music and concert programs). This also included investigating and recording the connections between the collection items and people and publishing these online. During this phase of the project, short biographies for known entertainers and composers who served with the AIF were to be written and published online, particularly those who had been identified as members of battalion bands.

The third phase involved the presentation of research for the *Music and the First World War* project in the form of a display in the Research Centre. This also included investigating possibilities for a data visualisation of the location of concerts, music performed, people involved and the music itself.

The fourth phase involved recording all the research produced in the First World War subject guide for future enquiries and digitisation projects, targeting the acquisition of specific sheet music titles not held in the collection and amending existing catalogue records if required.

This was the original project plan. In the end, some of the deliverables outlined above were consolidated in other ways or removed from the project altogether.

At the time that this project commenced, the Research Centre was digitising diaries and letters for the major First World War centenary project, *Anzac Connections*. The initial collections required for the *Music and the First World War* project were digitised as part of the *Anzac Connections* project. This included 26 collections of diaries and letters that had belonged to bandsmen, musically trained individuals or connections to the role of music in war. An additional 31 pieces of sheet music belonging to Ernest Nicholls, a performer with The Aussies Concert Party at Perham Downs during the First World War, were also included.

The digitisation of these collections started in October 2014. Part of this digitisation process required individually listing the contents of all selected collections down to item level and obtaining the appropriate copyright clearances. This listing process assisted with the discovery of the collections online. From beginning to end, given the complexities of some of these collections, the digitisation of these items took approximately 2 years to complete instead of the expected 6 months.

Among the collections digitised were the papers of Frank Reinhardt Fischer. Fischer was the brother of the Australian soprano Elsa Stralia who was performing in London during the First World War. He was also a talented singer and served with the 6th Battalion during the war. His collection of letters written to his family is full of references to well-known performers of the period, whom he met whenever he caught up with Elsa in England, and information about the concerts that he organised. On 29 July 1918, he wrote, 'there is no doubt that the Digger's enjoy a bit of music'.[4] Fischer was killed in France in September 1918.[5] After his death, Charles Gould mentioned in a letter to Elsa Stralia, 'Frank was beloved by the whole of our battalion, his splendid disposition and his voice made him the friend of us all when we were resting out of the line, and when we were fighting the enemy, his fearlessness and courage won the admiration of everyone'.[6]

It was Hector McLarty, however, who really summed up the effect of music on Australian soldiers. McLarty arrived on Gallipoli during the landing on 25 April 1915 and remained until the evacuation from Gallipoli on 20 December 1915. He was awarded the Military Medal on 16 August 1917 for his actions and bravery in the field at Messines, Belgium. On 18 December 1916, after 2 years of active service with the 3rd Field Artillery Brigade, McLarty wrote:

> Inside the gun pit a warm cheery fire is burning. For the last four hours a phonograph has been enthralling us. The pit is an inviting spot ... Round one side sit six soldiers, drinking in the music as if it were the strains of a Celestial Band – to them it is. The glow of the fire reflects each face. Their appearance is not prepossessing, for dirt has seamed their faces and their ragged mud-splattered clothes are wonderful to behold. Each face has its different characteristics, but for all the moment, bear that far away look which indicates thoughts of home. Personally, I am enthralled. The phonograph has taken hold of my heart strings. You see we have been on the Somme for a long while. It has been pretty rough. I hope I never see another eight weeks like it. We are tired and just about at the end of our strength and a touch of music sends me half mad.[7]

Only some of the 31 pieces that had belonged to Ernest Nicholls were included in the 100 songs that were digitised and then professionally recorded for this project. The bulk of the 100 pieces selected for the *Music and the First World War* project were digitised as an exhibition support project for the planned display in the Research Centre reading room.

At this time, the Memorial had a well-established procedure for clearing the copyright of unpublished archival records for digitising and publishing online, although not so much for published sheet music, and certainly not for recording this music. A new process for copyright clearances was required for this project. This involved liaising with the Australasian Performing Rights Association (APRA) to confirm the status of the songs selected and contacting publishing houses directly. In some instances, this required contacting publishing houses that had assumed the operations of long-defunct publishing houses. It was frustrating to find a great story about a song, confirm that it was held in the collection and then discover that it was still in copyright. This happened several times and each occurrence entailed a return to the drawing board. Eventually, a list of 100 songs was confirmed for the project. A list of some of these can be seen in Figure 3.

The pieces that were recorded were primarily selected due to references in diaries and letters written by soldiers from the First World War period or mentions in concert programs from the period. Others were selected if there was a strong story associated with the item or if it was representative of the sentiments of the period. Also selected were songs that were either written by a soldier serving in the Australian Imperial Force or which were owned by someone who used particular copies of the music during the war. There were also some songs selected because they were mentioned in Australian newspapers during the First World War period.

As you can imagine, these songs are quite different to the songs that we sing today but it was thought that these songs should be shared with a new generation of listeners so that they would not be forgotten. Some were, indeed, very much a product of their time but the majority confirmed that a good song is always a good song, even over 100 years later. Songs like 'A

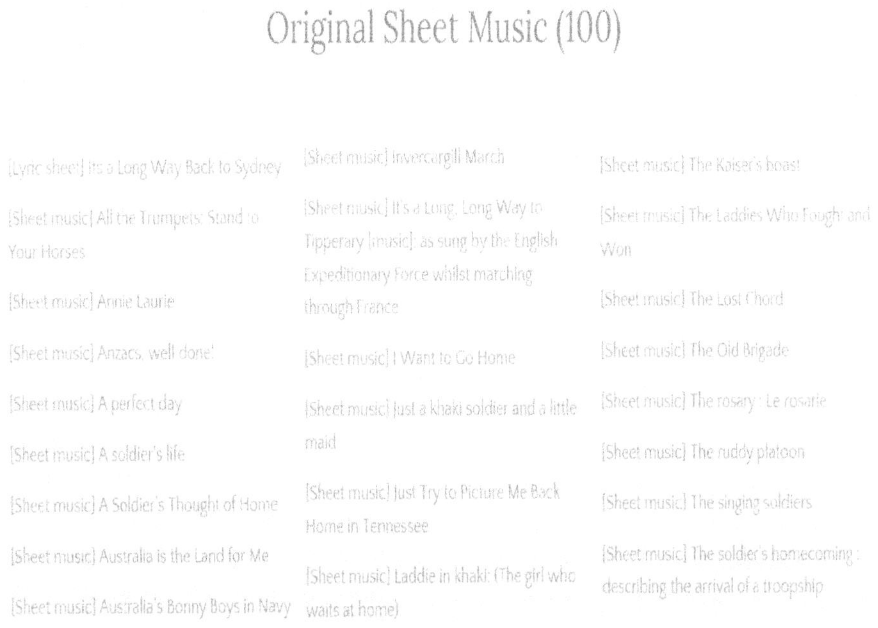

Original Sheet Music (100)

[Lyric sheet] It's a Long Way Back to Sydney

[Sheet music] All the Trumpets: Stand to Your Horses

[Sheet music] Annie Laurie

[Sheet music] Anzacs, well done!

[Sheet music] A perfect day

[Sheet music] A soldier's life

[Sheet music] A Soldier's Thought of Home

[Sheet music] Australia is the Land for Me

[Sheet music] Australia's Bonny Boys in Navy

[Sheet music] Invercargill March

[Sheet music] It's a Long, Long Way to Tipperary [music] as sung by the English Expeditionary Force whilst marching through France

[Sheet music] I Want to Go Home

[Sheet music] Just a khaki soldier and a little maid

[Sheet music] Just Try to Picture Me Back Home in Tennessee

[Sheet music] Laddie in khaki (The girl who waits at home)

[Sheet music] The Kaiser's boast

[Sheet music] The Laddies Who Fought and Won

[Sheet music] The Lost Chord

[Sheet music] The Old Brigade

[Sheet music] The rosary – Le rosarie

[Sheet music] The ruddy platoon

[Sheet music] The singing soldiers

[Sheet music] The soldier's homecoming : describing the arrival of a troopship

Figure 3. Selection of titles featured in the Music and the First World War project.[8]

Figure 4. MimsyXG database interface showing different modules.

perfect day', which was written by Carrie Jacobs-Bond in 1909, published in 1910 and enormously popular during the First World War period. The lyrics of this song relate sitting with your thoughts as the sun sets, reflecting on the joys of the day and saying farewell to friends. The song was performed by the composer herself at American training camps during the First World War.[9] The song went on to be described by some as the song of the 20th century, with reports that when it was at the height of its popularity it was not possible to go to a party in Australia without someone playing it or another of Jacobs-Bond's songs at the end of the evening to signal that it was time for guests to leave.[10] Jacobs-Bond is reported to have become the first female to make a million dollars from her music and she wrote the lyrics to this song while visiting friends in California.[11] It was 3 months later, while driving across the Mojave Desert, that she came up with the melody.[12]

The collection management system that supported the project was the museum collection management system known as **Mimsy XG** (Figure 4). This database consists of several modules that inter-connect and allow links to be made between catalogue records, media records and people records. This database was also the Memorial's main means of publishing collection data on the web, so getting a framework that delivered the original project concept was crucial.

This project included items from across three curatorial areas of the Memorial:

(1) Published Collections who manage the sheet music
(2) Sound Collections who manage the audio recordings
(3) Digitised Collections who manage the digitisation of the sheet music

Each of these curatorial areas required their own catalogue record for their derivative of each song title. This culminated in a total of 300 catalogue records.

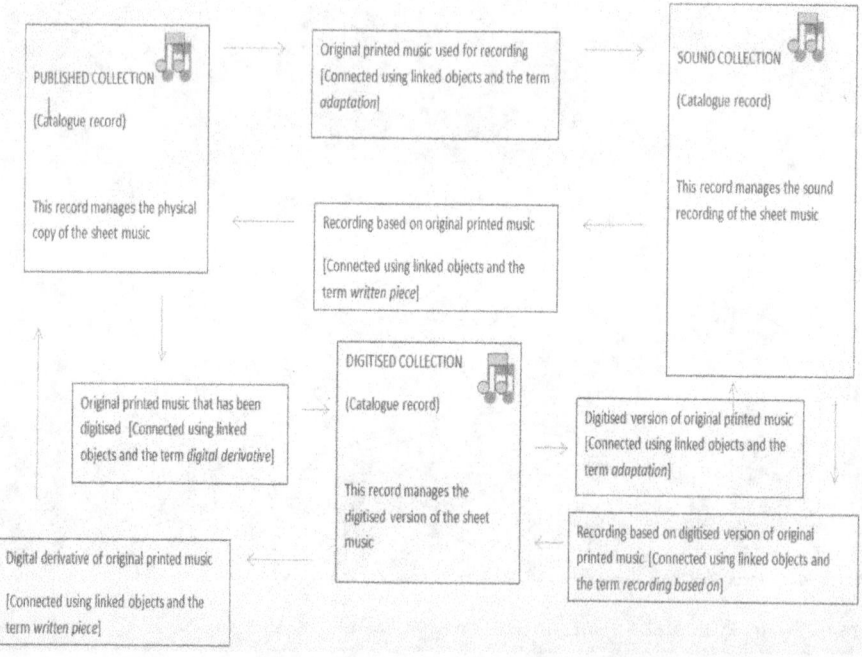

Figure 5. Database linkage model developed for catalogue records in MimsyXG.

The project team brought a variety of skills together to produce the project with some members having musical knowledge and others exhibiting technical skills with the database. The project required developing a model to explain the linkages to be made in MimsyXG (Figure 5) between catalogue records for the sound recordings, the digitised version of the sheet music and the physical copy of the sheet music. This was easier said than done as there were five versions of this model created before it was adopted. The reason for this was the intricacies of the project objective and its representation in the collection management database.

Each of these parts would have its own catalogue record and be linked together. The three catalogue records are linked together using a specific field in MimsyXG and a phrase to explain the type of relationship. The chosen phrases were adaptation, written piece, digital derivative and recording based on.

These phrases were crucial to the publishing framework as they had to be unique in order to ensure that there was no impact on other parts of the collection management system or that catalogue records unrelated to the project were not included when the catalogue records were published online.

The database linkage model shown in Figure 6 illustrates the links for other supporting collections that added to the story of the selected pieces. Another model was developed to make these links. The aim was to clearly show the connections to each piece of sheet music. The biggest collections which related to the sheet music were the concert programs found in Published Collections. It was known that some people performed specific songs at particular concerts and that the programs for these concerts were held in the collection. These were linked to and from the relevant sheet music using the phrase 'Subject'.

A decision was made to not link performers directly to the sheet music catalogue records. It was felt that there was more flexibility in linking concert programs to the sheet music because in doing so, it was not implied that the digitised copy of the sheet music was used in the

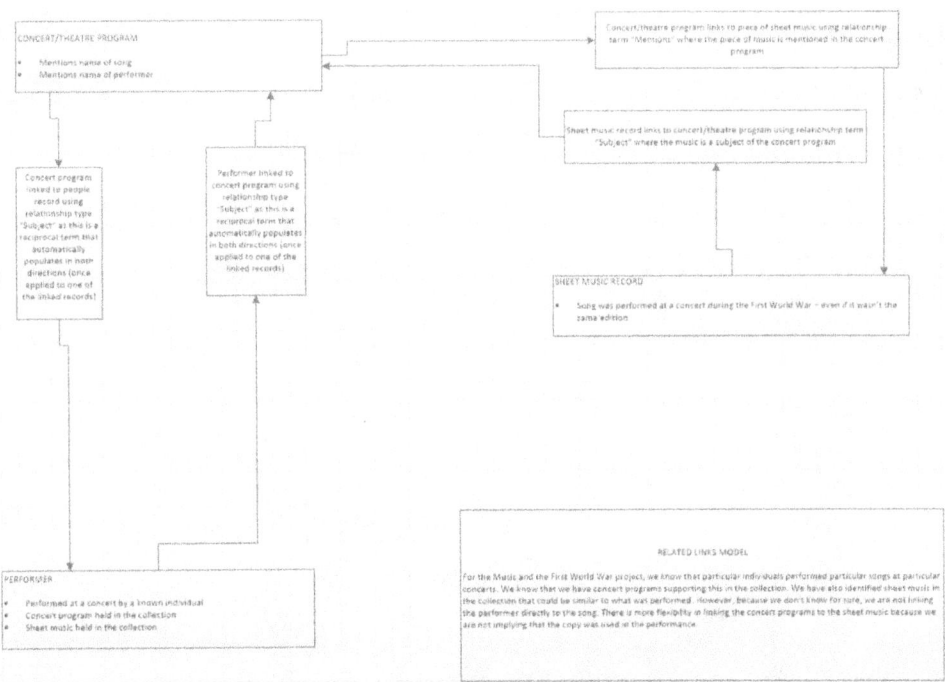

Figure 6. Database linkage model developed for supporting collections in MimsyXG.

rendition by each performer. These were linked to concert programs using the phrase 'subject'. The corresponding link from the concert programs used the phrase 'mentions'.

Some of these linkages became very complicated, but none more so than the database linkage model developed specifically for parodies. This model combined the existing two linkage models for catalogue records in MimsyXG. It defined the relationships between the physical collection record, the sound recording and the digital version as well as the related object, which is the parody. There were three parodies included in the project and each one of them required developing a visual model like the diagram in Figure 4, to ensure that the relationship phrases were entered correctly into the database.

The diagram in Figure 7 is the most complicated of the parody models as both the original song and the parody were recorded for 'It's a long, long way to Tipperary'. For 'It's a long way back to Sydney', four relationship phrases were required rather than the usual three, because it is based on a combination of original music and parody lyrics. Both had to be accounted for in the links. This diagram was originally created and used with different colours signifying the different catalogue records. For the purposes of this article, the diagram is in black and white. The top half relates to the original song 'It's a long, long way to Tipperary'. There are several boxes that include a relationship phrase of 'recording based on', 'subject', 'written piece' and 'adaptation', and these are linked back to other boxes representing the corresponding catalogue record. The bottom half relates to the parody titled 'It's a long way back to Sydney' and it also illustrates the relationship phrases adopted.

Originally, bright green squares showed the phrases used for the digital version, pale blue squares related to the sound recording and charcoal grey boxes related to the physical copy of the sheet music for 'It's a long, long was to Tipperary'. The mid-blue boxes related to phrases used in 'It's a long way back to Sydney', for the digital version, the bright yellow boxes related to the physical copy of the lyrics, and the pale green boxes related to the sound recording.

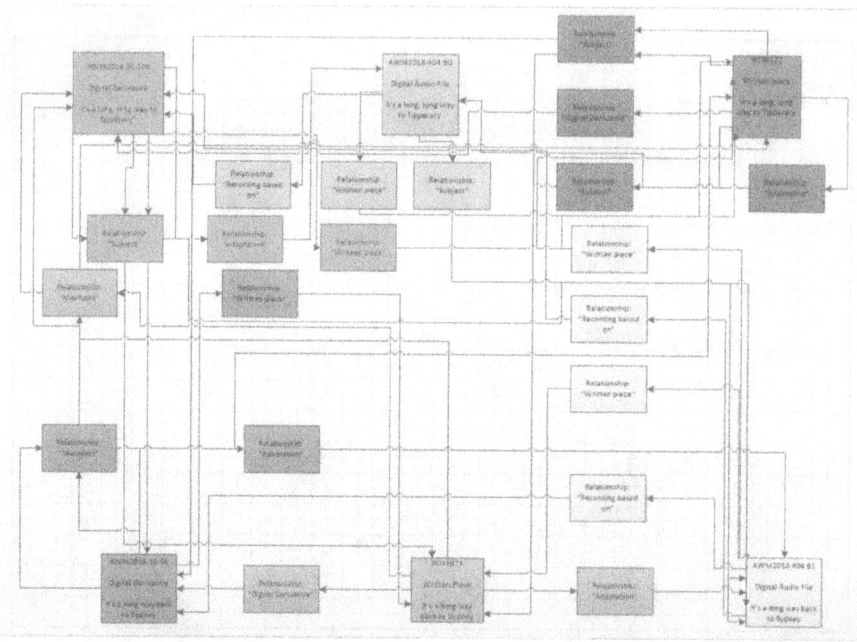

Figure 7. Parody Database Linkage Model showing linkages for the song 'It's a long, long way to Tipperary' and the parody 'It's a long way back to Sydney'.

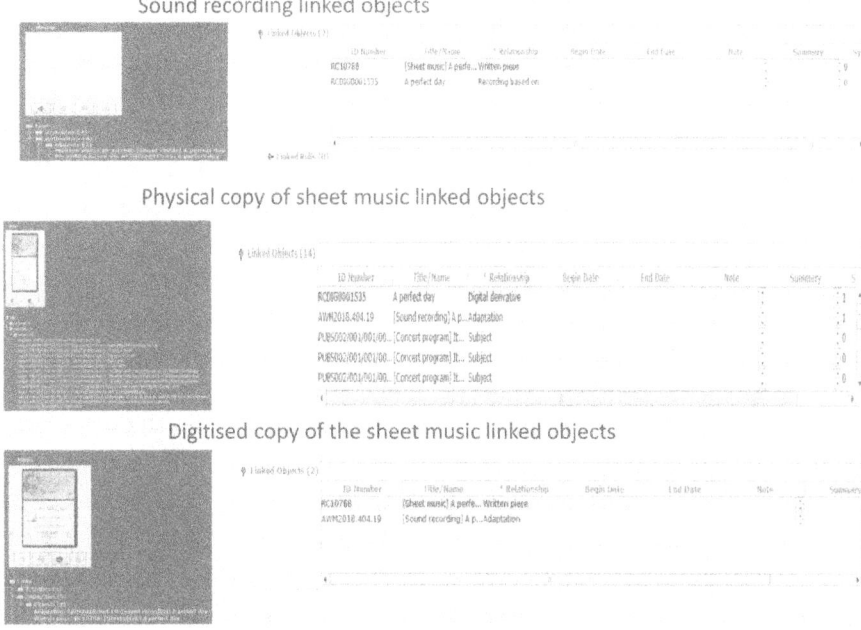

Figure 8. Linked object field collection database excerpts from catalogue records for 'A Perfect Day'.

As a side note, this parody became so popular that it was published in a Swedish magazine during 1915 and then re-published in an Australian newspaper for the Scandinavian migrant community.[13] Many soldiers were also sending the lyrics for the parody home in their letters, and these were also published by many local newspapers around Australia.[14]

The three individual models described above all came together in MimsyXG. Figure 8 features excerpts from the collection database showing the relationship phrases as they were used in the linked object field on the catalogue records for the classifications of Sound, Published Collections and Digitised Collection.

Figure 9. Media and linked media field excerpt from catalogue record for 'A Perfect Day'.

Figure 9 features an excerpt from the catalogue record for the physical copy of the sheet music for the song 'A perfect day'. Underneath the image, a highlighted box of a bell with sound and a camera can be seen. This indicates that media has been linked to the catalogue record.

One of the most important things achieved during this project relates back to the original concept of displaying the original sheet music and the sound recording together. This was not something that had been done for any project prior to this and it presented a new set of challenges. It was not known how to refer to a sound recording on a catalogue record that was just for a physical copy of the sheet music. Using the linked media functionality of MimsyXG, it was possible to combine the music and image all on the one record while still maintaining the links to other relevant records. However, as this was a new process, this meant changing the web rules so that the newly added images and Mp3 recording would show up on a record that was usually designed only for text.

The result of this was that the catalogue record for the physical version of each song now displays on the web with digital images of the sheet music displaying at the very top, ahead of information and a description of the physical copy. Underneath the description that includes information about the song and its composers is the historical description section that was created for this project. The historical description features information about performances of this song during the First World War and references the linked objects that mention the song such as concert programs and the individuals who performed the song during this period. There is also a link to download a copy of the sheet music and an embedded copy of the sound recording. An example of this can be seen in Figure 10 which

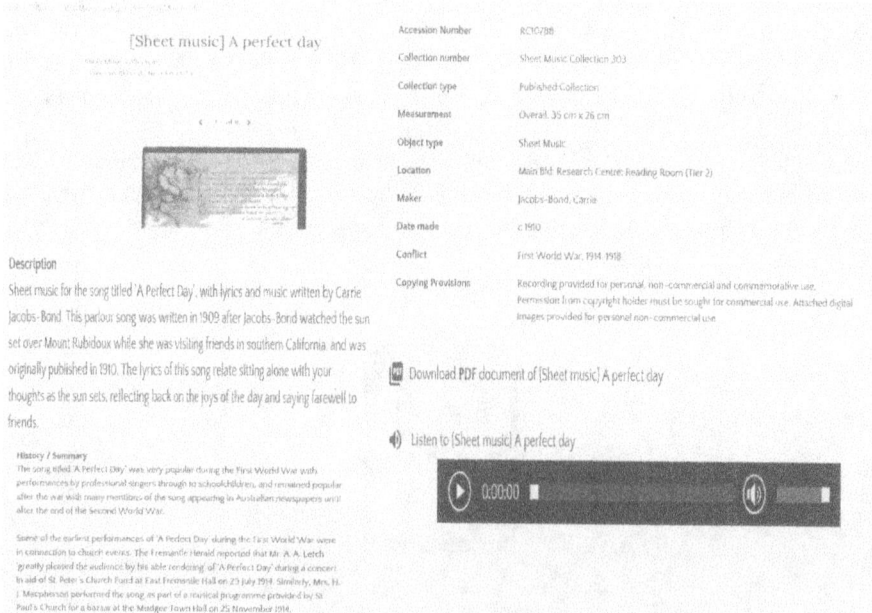

Figure 10. Elements that display on the online version of the catalogue record for the song 'A Perfect Day'.

shows the elements described above as they appear on the online version of the catalogue record for 'A Perfect Day'.

Another section of the online catalogue records for the Music and the First World War project is titled 'Related Information' (Figure 11). From here it is possible to click to the catalogue records for other items in the collection that reference this song and from those records, through to the biographies of some of the soldiers who performed these songs during the First World War. You can also click through to find more pieces of music held in the collection by each composer or find other songs that have similar themes or subjects.

One of the biggest benefits of this project beyond the ability to tell the stories of the performers, the history of these songs during the First World War period and the stories behind the writing of these songs, is that the project provided a means to do this and bring it all together in one location. It provided a means to place the songs in their social context during the First World War. It is possible to look at the songs and see which ones were most popular at welcome home events, which ones were popular for fundraising concerts and those that didn't really receive much attention. The project has also provided a vehicle to tell the stories of everyone involved in the writing and performing of these songs. People who have long been

Figure 11. Related information: objects, subjects and people for physical copy of the sheet music for 'A Perfect Day'.

Figure 12. Photograph of Corporal William Darwin, 7th Battalion, AIF taken in c1930s.[15]

forgotten and deserve to have their stories told. One of these people is Corporal William Darwin of the 7th Battalion who is pictured in Figure 12.

Notes

1. Australian War Memorial, Music and the First World War: 100 Years of Song, Online Exhibition, 04 November, Australian War Memorial, Online Exhibitions, 2019, available at https://www.awm.gov.au/visit/exhibitions-online/music-ww1, accessed 10 September 2021.
2. Australian War Memorial, [Sheet Music] 'Somewhere a Voice Is Calling', Digital Scan of Sheet Music, Australian War Memorial, Canberra, ACT, n.d., available at https://www.awm.gov.au/collection/C211529, accessed 21 September 2021.
3. Australian War Memorial, [Sheet Music] 'Give Me Dear Australia', Digital Scan of Sheet Music, Australian War Memorial, Canberra, ACT, n.d., available at https://www.awm.gov.au/collection/C239097, accessed 21 September 2021.
4. Frank Reinhardt Fischer, 'Letter from Frank Reinhardt Fischer to His Brother and Sister, France, 29 July 1918', Fischer, Frank Reinhardt (Lieutenant, b.1888 – d.1918), Australian War Memorial, 1918,

available at https://s3-ap-southeast-2.amazonaws.com/awm-media/collection/AWM2016.30.55/bundled/AWM2016.30.55.pdf, accessed 5 October 2022.
5. Australian War Memorial, Roll of Honour: Frank Reinhardt Fischer, Australian War Memorial, n.d., available at https://www.awm.gov.au/collection/R1731914, accessed 10 September 2021.
6. Charles Henry Gould, 'Letter of Condolence from Captain Charles Henry Gould to Elsa Stralia, France, 17 August 1918', Fischer, Frank Reinhardt (Lieutenant, b.1888 – d.1918), Australian War Memorial, 1918, available at https://s3-ap-southeast-2.amazonaws.com/awm-media/collection/AWM2016.30.56/bundled/AWM2016.30.56.pdf, accessed 10 September 2021.
7. Hector Roy McLarty, 'Typescript Copy of a Letter from Hector Roy McLarty, France, 18 December 1916', McLarty, Hector Roy, MM (Lieutenant), Australian War Memorial, 1916/1930, available at https://s3-ap-southeast-2.amazonaws.com/awm-media/collection/RCDIG0001555/bundled/RCDIG0001555.pdf, accessed 10 September 2021.
8. Australian War Memorial, Original Sheet Music (100), Australian War Memorial, n.d., available at https://www.awm.gov.au/webgroups/Original%20sheet%20music, accessed 21 September 2021.
9. Australian War Memorial, [Sheet Music] A Perfect Day, Australian War Memorial, n.d., available at https://www.awm.gov.au/collection/C211721, accessed 21 September 2021.
10. Ibid.
11. Ibid.
12. Ibid.
13. Australian War Memorial, [Lyric Sheet] Its a Long Way Back to Sydney, Australian War Memorial, n.d., available at https://www.awm.gov.au/collection/C1141469, accessed 21 September 2021.
14. Ibid.
15. 'Councillor Darwin', S6.3.1 – Album Projects (Photocopies), Victorian Bands' League Archive, Victoria, n.d. Sergeant William Darwin served during the First World War with the 7th Battalion, Australian Imperial Force and was also a member of the 7th Battalion Band. Darwin participated in the landing at Gallipoli on 25 April 1915 and served there until he was admitted to hospital on 18 September 1915. He had been buried by a shell explosion and dug out, unconscious, after 3 ½ hours. He wrote the poem, 'Anzacs, Well Done!' while recuperating in Scotland and returned to Australia in 1916. This poem became the lyrics for the song of the same name which was published about 1917. Australian War Memorial, Sergeant William Darwin, Australian War Memorial, Collection, n.d., available at https://www.awm.gov.au/collection/P11036419, accessed 21 September 2021.

www.ingramcontent.com/pod-product-compliance
Lightning Source LLC
Chambersburg PA
CBHW060421300426
44111CB00018B/2926